10-MINUTE FENG SHUI

10-MINUTE FENG SHUI

Easy Tips for Every Room

Skye Alexander

FAIR WINDS

P R E S S

GLOUCESTER MASSACHUSETTS

Text © Skye Alexander

First published in the USA by
Fair Winds Press
33 Commercial Street
Gloucester, MA 01930

Cover and book design by Jill Feron/Feron Design

ISBN 0-7394-2400-9

To Ron Conroy,
whose uncluttered lifestyle is truly awe-inspiring.

Contents

Introduction: Quick and Easy Feng Shui vii

Part One

Chapter 1: Feng Shui Basics 1
Chapter 2: What Does Your Home Say About You? 12
Chapter 3: Feng Shui Cures and Why They Work 29

Part Two

Chapter 4: Cures You Can Do in 10 Minutes or Less 47
    Prosperity 50
    Love 99
    Good Luck and Happiness 132
    Health/Well-Being 161

Chapter 5: Cures You Can Do in a Day or Less 172
    Prosperity 174
    Love 195
    Good Luck and Happiness 209
    Health/Well-Being 240

INTRODUCTION

QUICK AND EASY FENG SHUI

In the seventies and eighties, I worked as an interior designer. At that time, hardly anyone in the U.S. had heard of feng shui, the ancient Chinese art of placement. Yet most of the designers I knew were already using it instinctively. That's because good design is good feng shui (pronounced "fung shway"). Let me explain what I mean.

Despite its mystical trappings, much of feng shui is just common sense. For instance, when you enter a dark foyer you feel uncomfortable. Your first response is to turn on a light. In feng shui terms, you've implemented a "cure" by correcting an unpleasant situation. Here's another example. If you were to sit at your desk with your back to the door, you'd probably feel uneasy or distracted knowing that someone could come up behind you while you were busy working and startle you. If you reposition yourself so that you can see the door when you are seated at your desk, you'll feel more relaxed and can work more effectively.

So why does feng shui seem so complicated? Why are there so many books on the topic, each espousing different theories and practices?

Like every subject or field, feng shui has many levels, some practical and some esoteric. And like most philosophies—especially those that have evolved over a long period of time—feng shui has many different schools of thought which sometimes contradict or conflict with each other. Feng shui not only involves logical solutions to problems, it also uses symbols to influence the subconscious and some people find this perplexing. The Eastern consciousness itself, which underlies feng shui's imagery and concepts, is inherently confusing to many Westerners.

But you don't have to understand all the intricacies of feng shui to reap its benefits. I've found that most Westerners aren't particularly interested in plumbing the mysterious depths of ancient Chinese wisdom. They don't care about geomancy, the *I Ching*, or the green dragon who guards the East. They just want something that works.

HOW TO USE THIS BOOK

10-Minute Feng Shui is designed for busy, action-oriented Westerners who want quick results without a lot of bother. Many of the feng shui tips and solutions in Part Two can be implemented in ten minutes or less. The others shouldn't take longer than a day to complete. These tips are grouped into four categories: prosperity, love, good luck and happiness, and health/well-being. If you don't want to know anything much about feng shui or why it works, you can go directly to this section and get started.

If, on the other hand, you're the sort of person who likes to understand a bit about the tools you're using, Part One covers the basics of feng shui without getting too technical or philosophical. It also explains what your home says about you and how you can change your life by making changes in your home.

The most important factor in using feng shui successfully is your intent—the physical "cures" are only part of the process. You'll get better results if you truly want to correct a particular problem and believe what you are doing will work. In this way, feng shui is like any other endeavor—the more you put into it, the more you'll get back.

FENG SHUI BASICS

FENG SHUI, the ancient Chinese art of placement, is thousands of years old, yet until recently few people in the West knew anything about it. In 1987, when I went into a gift shop in Boston's Chinatown to buy my first bagua mirror, the Asian woman behind the counter looked at me as if I'd requested a black-market item and asked suspiciously, "How you know bagua?"

Although millions of Westerners have now heard of feng shui, most are still confused about how to use it. Books, magazines, and mail-order kits have raised as many questions as they've answered. Which school of feng shui is best? How can I evaluate my home in feng shui terms? What can I do if I live in an apartment and my options are limited? Does all this strange stuff really work?

To answer the last question first, yes, feng shui really works. And it works even if you don't understand or believe it, although in my experience results may take longer or be less successful if you approach feng shui with a closed mind. Regardless of your living circumstances, you can use feng shui. Few homes or apartments are ideal; most can benefit from some feng shui adjustments. Because there are so many ways to implement feng shui, it offers something for everyone and virtually any problem area can be rectified.

Feng shui lets you make your own "luck." Here in the West, we tend to view luck as pure chance, an inexplicable and quixotic force that's outside our control. The Chinese, however, believe luck can be cultivated and directed to enhance health, wealth, and happiness.

Much of feng shui focuses on using "cures." They're called cures because they remedy problems in your home and in your life. Part Two of this book offers hundreds of quick and easy cures you can implement to increase prosperity, enhance relationships, improve health, and attract good luck. But before we get to that, let's look briefly at some of the principles and concepts that underlie this deceptively simple system.

The objective of feng shui is to create harmony and balance in your environment. This involves applying practical solutions to everyday problems, such as establishing convenient traffic patterns through your home, positioning furniture in comfortable arrangements, and eliminating clutter in your living and work spaces. There's nothing magical about these cures—they are sensible ways to make life easier and more efficient.

Feng shui has an esoteric side as well, and this is the part that seems peculiar at first to Westerners. But once you understand a few basic tenets, it's really quite simple. Much of feng shui is based on symbolic associations. Some of these symbols also appear in other schools of thought such as numerology, dream analysis, and aromatherapy. For example, green is a color we connect with plants and healthy, growing things. It is also the color of paper money in some countries. So, in feng shui, green can be used symbolically to promote financial growth. (In chapter 3, I explain the most common feng shui cures, how to use them, and why they work.)

The most important part of feng shui, however, is your intention. When you put a cure in place, you demonstrate a willingness to take charge of your life and to change something that you don't like about it. Many cures work by helping you to focus on your goal—to make more money, attract a romantic partner, or improve your health. They succeed through the power of suggestion. Each time you look at the cure, you are reminded of your objective and your resolve is strengthened. In this sense, the cure has no real power in itself, it is merely a mental aid—your willpower is what makes feng shui work.

THE INSIDE STORY

As Karen Kingston writes in *Clear Your Clutter with Feng Shui*, "Feng shui is the art of balancing and harmonizing the flow of natural energies in our surroundings to create beneficial effects in our lives." It works on both a physical and a psychological level. According to feng shui philosophy, our inner and outer worlds are closely linked and they influence each other—they are two sides of the same coin, so to speak.

Our homes outwardly mirror our internal, emotional states. To the trained eye, your home reveals a great deal about you. If an area in your home is cluttered, for instance, you are probably experiencing confusion or blockages in the part of your life that corresponds to the cluttered section. Conversely, areas that you just naturally tend to keep neat and organized show the parts of your life that are functioning smoothly. According to feng shui, by cleaning away the physical clutter you can actually clear up the confusion and disorder in your life.

Here's a good example. A carpenter I know had a habit of putting his toolbox down just inside the door when he came home from work. He had to step over it to get into the house. Symbolically, he had placed an obstacle in his path. In his professional life, this man continually encountered blocks that impeded his success. Once he retrained himself to put his toolbox elsewhere, leaving the passageway into his home free and clear, many of his work-related problems disappeared.

Ch'i

Literally, feng shui means "wind" and "water." Like wind and water, it involves movement and circulation. The goal is to direct ch'i—a vital energy that animates all life—through your environment so that its movement resembles a gently flowing stream or a pleasant breeze.

According to Chinese belief, ch'i (pronounced "chee") flows through everything: the earth, the atmosphere, our homes, our bodies. Practitioners of Eastern medicine maintain that health problems arise when the body's ch'i becomes blocked. Acupuncturists, for example, clear away blockages in the body's energetic system so ch'i can flow smoothly and restore health. It's a bit like unclogging a pipe so water can run freely through it again.

That's what we do in feng shui, too—we remove obstructions in the home that are interfering with the proper circulation of ch'i. When ch'i gets stuck in our living and working spaces, we experience the adverse effects in a variety of ways. Finances may languish, relationships with other people may be limited or unfulfilling, health may become impaired.

Ch'i that moves too rapidly can also cause problems. Money may go out as quickly as it comes in, relationships may be unsettled, tension may damage health. By using feng shui cures, we can direct the movement of ch'i through our homes and workplaces so that it nurtures our lives and brings us what the Chinese call the Three Great Blessings: health, wealth, and happiness.

Ch'i moves through your home in much the same way as you do. If you can walk comfortably through the different rooms of your home, it will be easy for ch'i to circulate smoothly and harmoniously. If, on the other hand, you must continually walk around awkwardly placed furniture, architectural obstructions, and clutter, ch'i will have a hard time getting through, too.

YIN AND YANG

Many cosmologies perceive the world as embodying two complementary forces: masculine and feminine. In the East, these fundamental energies are called yin (feminine) and yang (masculine). According to feng shui philosophy, these primordial forces are omnipresent, existing everywhere, in everything. They are entwined and interdependent—neither can exist without the other. Our goal, in working with these energies, is to create balance so that neither force dominates.

Yin is considered to be yielding, receptive, inner-directed; yang is assertive, active, and outer-oriented. The yin force is present in darkness, water, silence, curved shapes, cool colors. Yang abides in light, fire, noise, sharp lines, bright colors. Yin energy is restful; yang is stimulating. When you combine these two polar

energies in your home in an even-handed manner, you create a comfortable, harmonious environment. If, as you look around your home, you notice a preponderance of either yin or yang in a room, you can counteract its influence by adding its opposite.

In some cases you may want to emphasize either yin or yang, in order to produce conditions that support your intention. For example, you might choose to let the yin force dominate in a bedroom to create a peaceful, quiet space. To accomplish this, you could paint the bedroom blue or green, install low-level lighting, and decorate with soft, curved furniture. Conversely, in an exercise room, you'd probably want to accentuate the yang force to stimulate vitality and activity. To do this, you might include orange or red in your color scheme, play upbeat music, and illuminate the room with bright lighting.

THE FIVE ELEMENTS

A fundamental concept in Chinese philosophy holds that the world is comprised of five elements—fire, earth, water, wood, and metal—and that everything consists of one or more of these elements. The five elements are one of the basic building blocks of Chinese medicine as well as feng shui. According to Chinese belief, each of these elements depicts a different aspect of ch'i. By incorporating the five elements in your environment in a harmonious way, you can bring balance into your life.

Each of these elements is present in many forms, all around us. Not merely physical substances, the elements are energetic forces that permeate our universe. Colors, materials, shapes, scents, and activities all can be linked with one element or another. Interior designers often blend these elements in a beneficial way without realizing it, simply because doing so creates a pleasing result.

Each element operates in its own, unique way and produces a specific effect. Fire stimulates, earth stabilizes, water softens and blends, wood expands, metal strengthens and concentrates. Too much fire in a room can cause tension and instability; too much metal can result in rigidity. If, as you look around your home, you notice a preponderance of one element in a room, you can counteract its influence by adding items that correspond to the other elements.

In much the same way as you might prepare a recipe, you can combine and adjust the elements in your home or workplace any way you choose in order to bring about the conditions you desire. For example, add metal objects to children's bedrooms to help them focus on their studies; add wooden items in a home office to encourage business and financial growth.

You don't have to be a feng shui master to incorporate the five elements auspiciously in your home. The table on the next page shows which things fall into which elemental category. Your goal is to combine the elements in your living environment so that all are represented and no single element overwhelms the others.

ELEMENTAL TABLE

	Fire	Earth	Water	Wood	Metal
Colors	• red • orange	• brown • yellow	• black • dark blue	• green • blue	• white • gray
Materials	• electricity	• brick • stone • ceramic	• glass	• wood • paper	• metal
Shapes	• triangle	• square	• wavy • irregular	• rectangle	• round • oval
Household Objects	• candles • fireplace • stove • TV • stereo • lighting • computer • heat	• masonry • marble • tile • pottery	• sink • tub • toilet • faucets • aquarium • pool • glass items • plumbing	• plants • wood items • books	• pots & pans • silverware • appliances • metal items • metallic finishes

THE TAO

Feng shui is based on the concept that all of life is interconnected. This connectedness is expressed in the spiritual philosophy known as Taoism. The Tao (pronounced "dow"), or "the Way," teaches that in order to be happy, we must learn to live in harmony with nature and our environment, with the universal energies that are present all around us in the heavens and the earth. As Sarah Rossbach explains in *Interior Design with Feng Shui*, "Tao is a process and a principle linking man with the Universe." Although it is said that the true Tao cannot be known, in essence, the Tao is the centering principle that holds together the whole of existence, both that which we can see and that which is unseen.

That's a bit esoteric and vague for most people—and you certainly don't have to subscribe to the tenets of Taoism to use feng shui effectively. Feng shui does incorporate many aspects of the Tao into its cures, however. One of the most obvious ways is by bringing plants, stones, water, fish, and other representations of the natural world into the home. Aquariums and fountains, for instance, are popular feng shui cures—undoubtedly, you've seen aquariums in Chinese restaurants, where they are believed to bring good luck. Plants, which offer visual appeal and help to cleanse the air of carbon dioxide, are one of the most frequently used remedies in feng shui.

Other cures imitate nature in order to subtly remind us of our link with the environment. For example, you could adjust the lighting in your home so that it emanates from various sources at different intensity levels, pooling and dappling on your floor, walls, and furnishings in much the same way as sunlight filters through the trees in a forest. Or, you could install a ceiling fan to circulate air currents about your home to suggest a gentle breeze. When we get to Part Two, you'll notice that many of the cures draw on nature in an attempt to create a sense of connectedness and an awareness of human life as part of the greater whole that is the Tao.

FENG SHUI AND INTUITION

Many of the cures and techniques used in feng shui are logical, physical ones—rearranging furniture into comfortable seating groups, for instance, or fixing a window that doesn't open properly. But feng shui also operates on the subconscious or intuitive level. Even things we aren't consciously aware of still have an impact on the subconscious. If certain factors in your environment cause discomfort at a subconscious dimension, your outer, conscious life will be adversely affected, too.

Once you start paying attention to your feelings and responses whenever you enter a space, you will begin to understand the ambient energies that are present. Have you ever entered a room and felt "bad vibes" even though you couldn't pinpoint the cause? That's how ch'i responds, too. It is drawn to pleasing, harmonious environments and repelled by discordant ones.

Try to attune yourself to the subtle energies and vibrations that exist in various environments. Trust your impressions and let them guide you as you apply feng shui in your home or workplace. After awhile, you'll be able to sense that you've done the right thing, because it feels right.

CHAPTER 2

WHAT DOES YOUR HOME SAY ABOUT YOU?

WHEN A PALM READER looks at your hand, she

sees your life reflected in the lines and mounds on your palm and fingers. Each mark says something about you—your personality, your experiences, your attitudes, your health. A feng shui master sees you mirrored in your home; he can tell what's going on in your life simply by examining the condition of your living space.

Clutter, as I mentioned before, is synonymous with confusion and blockages. Broken furniture can signify broken dreams, physical injuries, or breaks in communication between family members. Doors or windows that stick may represent areas of your life that are stuck.

In feng shui, each sector of your home corresponds to a particular part of your life. The condition of the different areas will show which aspects of your life are in good shape and which ones need a little TLC. For instance, your living room may be quite clean, orderly, and inviting, but your study is piled high with clutter. A feng shui master might interpret this to mean that you are content with your social life, but are having problems with your career and/or finances. You can correct any areas that aren't functioning smoothly by applying the appropriate feng shui cures.

Here's a personal example to illustrate. When I first moved to the town where I now live, I felt lonely and isolated. I wanted to meet new friends and expand my social circle. At that time, the sector of my home that relates to friendship contained an artfully arranged cluster of dried tree branches—an apt symbol of my rather barren social life. To remedy the situation, I replaced the dead, leafless branches with a large, live plant. Before long, I began meeting new people. I now enjoy rewarding friendships with a diverse and interesting group of men and women, and entertain in my home often.

Feng shui considers our homes and workplaces to be living entities. Each feature in a building corresponds to a part of the human body. The front door, for instance, is the "mouth" of the building. Windows are its "eyes." Ch'i enters through these openings. Halls and passageways in a building can be likened to the body's veins and arteries—they are the conduits through which ch'i travels as it circulates from room to room. A building's electrical system is similar to the human neurological system. Plumbing is the functional equivalent of our elimination system. Wall studs, beams, and other structural supports relate to our bones. When one of these features in your home is damaged or malfunctioning, it can signal problems in the corresponding part of your body.

ANALYZING YOUR HOME

Feng shui has many schools of thought and each one approaches the subject somewhat differently. Consequently, there is much debate about which version of feng shui is best and this results in a great deal of confusion. In the West, the two best-known feng shui systems are the Compass School and the Black Hat School. The Compass system establishes balance by aligning energies with the eight compass directions. Black Hat feng shui uses an octagon-shaped tool called a bagua to divide a space into eight sectors, each of which relates to a specific area of life (such as wealth, fame, or relationships).

However, these systems are somewhat complex and can be difficult for some people to grasp. Although I don't deny the validity of these schools—and others that are less popular—the objective of this book is to demystify feng shui and make it accessible to everyone. Therefore, I offer a less complicated yet still effective method for applying feng shui in your own home or workplace. This easy system links each room of your home with an area of your life, based on the room's primary purpose. For example, the living room is used for socializing, so it corresponds to your social life, friendships, and leisure activities. The bedroom is a place for privacy and intimacy, so it's associated with love relationships. The study, where work is performed, relates to money and career.

Undoubtedly some readers and feng shui practitioners will disagree with the ideas and methodology I present here. I urge you to experiment to see what works for you, while paying attention to your feelings and impressions. Your increased awareness over time will help you understand how ch'i operates in your own environment, so you can put into place the feng shui adjustments and cures that are right for you.

Front Entrance

The front door of your home is its mouth. Ch'i enters here and nourishes your home, in much the same way as food is taken into your body as nourishment. A large, distinctive, easily accessible front door allows more ch'i into your home than one that is small, dark, or difficult to find. Have you ever noticed how mansions usually have grand entrances? They welcome positive ch'i to come inside, filling the home with abundance of all kinds.

An attractive entryway not only invites ch'i and visitors into your home, it also gives the public a favorable image of you. Therefore, it's important to make the entrance to your home—including the sidewalk, porch, front steps, yard, et cetera—as appealing as possible. Because this is the point at which ch'i first enters your home, problems with your entryway that limit ch'i's access will adversely affect all areas of your life.

Common Sense Feng Shui Tips to Improve Your Front Entrance

❖ Clear away any clutter or obstacles that could obstruct access to your front door.

❖ Install adequate lighting so your entrance is clearly visible.

❖ Keep your entryway in good repair—fix loose steps or a broken doorbell and make sure the door opens easily.

❖ Paint your front door an eye-catching color and attach shiny brass numbers and hardware to it.

Foyer/Entrance Hall

The space just inside the front door is also important, for this area welcomes ch'i to flow into the rest of your home and fill it with positive energy. The foyer operates in conjunction with the exterior portion of your home's entrance, facilitating the movement of ch'i through your living space. If ch'i is obstructed or impaired at this point, its ability to energize every area of your life—health, wealth, relationships, et cetera—will be limited.

To understand how ch'i responds, pay attention to your own reactions as you enter different buildings. If a home's foyer or front hallway is dark, cluttered, or claustrophobic, you'll probably feel awkward, unsure about whether to retreat or continue on into the other parts of the home. But notice how a well-lit, cheerful entrance area makes you feel welcome and comfortable.

If you encounter a wall immediately upon entering, you'll feel blocked. This is how ch'i responds, too. To correct the problem, hang a picture with a distant view there to symbolically expand the area beyond its confining, physical dimensions. Split-entry foyers, which feature a stairway going to an upper level and another leading down to a lower level, can be confusing to ch'i—it doesn't know which way to flow. Direct ch'i into one area or the other by illuminating the path you want it to take or accentuating one stairway with artwork, plants, or other visually appealing cures.

Common Sense Feng Shui Tips to Improve Your Foyer

❖ Install adequate lighting.

❖ Paint your entrance area a sunny color such as yellow or peach.

❖ Eliminate any clutter that could impede progress into the rest of the home.

❖ Keep stairs, doors, and architectural features in good condition.

❖ Provide a convenient place for people entering and leaving your home to put their coats, keys, eyeglasses, umbrellas, and other articles.

❖ Neatly organize your front hall closet.

LIVING ROOM

In most homes, the foyer adjoins the living room. Many apartments and small houses, however, dispense with a separate entrance area so that you come directly into the living room upon entering the home. If the entryway into your home is clear and inviting, ch'i will naturally flow smoothly into this space. To keep ch'i moving freely, make sure the pathway into your living room is unobstructed by furniture, clutter, doors, or other barriers.

Because the living room is the part of the home where you usually entertain guests and where the home's occupants tend to come together to socialize, this room is connected with your social life. The condition of this room will affect your friendships, social life, and relationships with people in your community. A cheerful, comfortable living room encourages positive social interactions and rewarding friendships. A barren, dark, or cramped living room limits your ability to make and enjoy other people's company; a cluttered living area can produce confusion, obstacles, or disagreements with companions.

The "main" room in the home, the living room has a profound effect on the general happiness, good fortune, and well-being of its inhabitants. Therefore, it's important to keep this area clean, orderly, and in good condition. Decorate it as attractively as possible so that it conveys a sense of comfort and ease, inviting guests and family members to relax here.

Common Sense Feng Shui Tips to Improve Your Living Room

❖ Arrange furniture so that, when seated, no one's back is to the room's entrance. This makes it easy for everyone to see and greet whoever comes into the room, so that guests feel welcome.

❖ Don't position a sofa or other large piece of furniture so near the room's entrance that it blocks passage into your living area.

- ❖ Configure seating into "conversation groups" that enable people to communicate easily with each other, without having to shout or lean forward to converse.

- ❖ Keep passageways through the room clear so you can conveniently move about the space to open windows or access closets.

- ❖ Provide a variety of lighting sources, for reading, ambiance, and other activities.

THE KITCHEN

The kitchen is the room where meals are prepared, so this area provides nourishment for the home's inhabitants. From the perspective of feng shui, the kitchen is connected with your prosperity and its condition reveals a great deal about your financial situation. A clean, efficient kitchen suggests that you are comfortable with money matters and aren't troubled by financial woes. A disorganized, dirty, or poorly operating kitchen indicates confusion, difficulties, or conflicts where money is concerned. Cures to attract wealth, therefore, are frequently implemented in the kitchen.

A large, well-appointed, and attractive kitchen is generally advantageous to the inhabitants' wealth. But your kitchen needn't be grand or filled with the latest appliances and gadgets to have a beneficial impact on your finances. What's important is that your kitchen is neat and orderly, and that everything in it works properly.

In feng shui terms, the stove is the focal point of the kitchen. This is where food is prepared and money is generated. If possible, position the stove so that the cook can interact with other people in the kitchen and his/her back is not to the kitchen's entrance. Try not to cram the stove into a corner, where the cook will feel constrained while working as this can limit your money-making options. From a design perspective, it's a good idea to configure the stove, sink, and refrigerator in a triangular pattern so that it's easy for the cook to move from one work zone to the other as s/he prepares food.

Make sure your stove is in good working order. If the heating elements are burned out, your wealth-producing capabilities will be diminished and you may run into financial difficulties. When you clean your stove, you symbolically clear the way for prosperity to come into your life and demonstrate your willingness to invest effort and energy into improving your finances.

Common Sense Feng Shui Tips to Improve Your Kitchen

❖ Install adequate lighting as a safety measure as well as to attract ch'i.

❖ Use your stove regularly to generate wealth.

❖ Keep the passageways through your kitchen clear to prevent accidents and allow ch'i to flow smoothly.

- ❖ Organize cabinets and closets to improve efficiency and reduce clutter that can produce confusion or discord.

- ❖ Make sure all appliances are functioning properly to reduce frustration and waste.

- ❖ Keep your kitchen clean to prevent health risks and financial decay.

Dining Room

Situated between the kitchen and the living room, the dining room combines the qualities of these other two rooms in practical as well as symbolic terms. In an obvious sense, we nourish ourselves and interact socially in the dining room. From the perspective of feng shui, the dining room's condition provides clues to understanding both your social life and your finances.

If you don't eat in your dining room very often, you may experience limited social activity or stagnant finances (unless your kitchen, living room, and/or study indicate otherwise). A cluttered dining room—especially one that is also used for other purposes—can suggest confusion, stress, or discord in both areas of your life. If your goal is to improve either your social life or your financial picture, you can apply feng shui cures in your dining room as well as in the kitchen and/or living room.

The dining room also affects your health, because food is consumed and digested here. A peaceful, congenial environment is conducive to good digestion, therefore some feng shui cures for your dining room are designed to promote harmony. A round table is a good choice if you want to encourage togetherness and cooperation among family members or to improve relationships with friends or business colleagues because circles represent unity and wholeness. Rectangles, because they are longer than they are wide, suggest movement and growth—use a rectangular table if your goal is to attract wealth or increase your vitality. (I'll talk more about the symbolism of shapes in chapter 3.)

What you eat and how you serve meals are also important considerations. Pay attention to colors, aromas, tastes, and ambiance as all of these factors contribute to your health, wealth, and happiness.

Of course, many apartments and some small homes don't have dining rooms. This doesn't mean you won't have any friends or money. Simply apply the appropriate feng shui cures in the area of your home where you eat meals.

Common Sense Feng Shui Tips to Improve Your Dining Room

❖ Don't eat on the run or do work while you are eating.

❖ Avoid arguments during meals, which can upset digestion.

❖ Don't watch TV during meals—focus on interacting with your fellow diners.

- ❖ Clear away clutter that can undermine positive relationships with other people or inhibit the flow of wealth into your life.

- ❖ Repair broken furniture that could lead to breaks with friends or business colleagues.

- ❖ If possible, arrange seating so no one's back is to the dining room's entrance.

BEDROOM

Because we spend about one-third of our lives in our bedrooms, these are important parts of our homes and they have a profound influence on us. A bedroom reveals a great deal about the person who sleeps there—particularly regarding his or her private life, as the bedroom is the place where private, intimate activities (sleeping, dressing, making love) occur. A comfortable, attractive bedroom contributes to a happy love life. A cluttered bedroom suggests confusion or discord in a relationship. Broken or worn furnishings can signify breaks in communication, unfulfilled dreams, or a relationship that has lost its luster.

When I was in the process of getting divorced, one of the drawers in my bedroom dresser became stuck shut—I couldn't even open it enough to fix it. Some time later, when I got involved in a new relationship, the drawer suddenly opened up on its own.

Additionally, the bedroom is linked with health, for it is here that we rest and rejuvenate ourselves each night, and where we retire when we're ill. Some feng shui cures to improve health are implemented in the bedroom.

Ideally, the bed should be positioned so that you have a clear view of the door when you are in bed. Subconsciously, this makes you feel more at ease because you can see anyone who enters the bedroom. But if your bed is too close to the door, you may be disturbed by noises outside your bedroom or feel you don't have enough privacy. Nor is it a good idea to place your bed directly under a window, where drafts can cause discomfort or illness.

Common Sense Feng Shui Tips to Improve Your Bedroom

❖ Clear passageways through your bedroom to enhance health and love relationships.

❖ Position your bed away from the door, but where you'll have a clear view of the door so your sleep won't be disturbed.

❖ Don't store things under your bed, as clutter can have an adverse effect on romantic relationships.

❖ Repair broken furnishings to prevent breaks in a relationship.

❖ Install dimmer switches on lamps so you can adjust lighting to suit your mood.

BATHROOM

The bathroom and your home's plumbing system correspond to your elimination system. It is here that personal cleansing rituals take place and where wastes are flushed away. However, ch'i can also be flushed out of your home via the toilet and bathroom drains. Therefore, it's important to minimize opportunities for ch'i to flow out of your home too quickly, taking your prosperity along with it. Faucets that drip or a toilet that runs aren't just wasteful, they can cause money to slowly leak away. The Chinese believe that even open, visible drains tend to suck ch'i—and wealth—out of your home. To prevent this, close toilet lids and shower curtains.

A place for purification, the bathroom is also connected with your health. In an obvious sense, germs can collect in a bathroom that is dirty or in bad repair. In feng shui terms, your vitality can be sapped if ch'i disappears down the drain too quickly. The strong yin force that water generates is likely to dominate in the bathroom, producing an imbalance that can dampen your physical energy. Bright lighting adds the yang component and can help offset this imbalance, while also making it easier to shave, apply makeup, and perform other personal care functions.

Common Sense Feng Shui Tips to Improve Your Bathroom

❖ Keep your bathroom clean, neat, and orderly.

❖ Close toilet lids and shower curtains to conceal water outlets and keep ch'i—and money—from going down the drain.

❖ Repair leaky faucets, shower heads, and toilets to prevent waste.

❖ Install adequate lighting for convenience and yin/yang balance.

STUDY/HOME OFFICE

Offices and workspaces in the home have become increasingly common in recent years, as more people work out of their homes or bring work home with them. As you might expect, a study or work area in your home relates to your career and finances. From the perspective of feng shui, the condition of this room describes your attitudes toward money, your ability to attract wealth, your career goals, and your overall work situation.

A cluttered, disorganized office suggests confusion, obstacles, or stress in connection with money and/or your job. If your work area is jammed with lots of "stuff" you may have trouble attracting new opportunities or money—there's no room for anything more to enter your life. An office that is neat, clean, and orderly, on the other hand, indicates clarity regarding your career goals and finances. Broken or damaged furnishings or equipment can symbolize breaks in communication, deals that fall through, or financial losses.

Ideally, you'll want to position your desk or work station so that when you are seated at it you can easily see the entrance to your office. If your back is to the door, you may feel uneasy or have difficulty concentrating because someone could come up behind you and startle you when you are working.

Common Sense Feng Shui Tips to Improve Your Study/Workspace

❖ Place your desk so you can easily see the entrance to your office.

❖ Install good lighting so you can see clearly. This will also increase the amount of ch'i in your work area and enhance your vitality.

❖ Eliminate clutter to make room for money and opportunities to come into your life.

CHAPTER 3

FENG SHUI CURES
AND
WHY THEY WORK

SOME FENG SHUI CURES are practical, such as

positioning your furniture in comfortable seating arrangements. Others are symbolic, such as placing a circular area rug on your floor to promote harmony among family members. Many remedies, however, combine practical and symbolic aspects and therefore work on both levels.

A circular dining or conference table is a good example. This is considered to be the friendliest shape because it eliminates the hierarchical "head" and "foot" positions characteristic of a rectangular table. Additionally, people seated around a circular table can see and converse with each other more easily than they could at a rectangular one. Studies have shown that when people sit at a round table, they are more likely to exercise give-and-take and compromise than when they sit at a rectangular table, hence the term "round table discussion." The circle's symbolism—harmony and unity—is reiterated in functional terms.

Eliminating clutter, which is one of the most powerful and common feng shui cures, is both practical and symbolic. From a practical standpoint, when your home or office is neat and orderly, you can work more efficiently and effectively. As a result, this cure helps you become more prosperous. Symbolically, getting rid of old things you no longer need opens up space for new riches to come into your life. The Universe, it's said, abhors a vacuum and will immediate begin to fill it.

Here's an amusing story of how feng shui "decluttering" brought an immediate financial reward to a California woman. This woman tends to be a bit of a pack rat. The drawers in her kitchen were crammed with all sorts of stuff—so much, in fact, that some of them no longer opened and she couldn't even remember what was in them. When a mutual friend of ours (who is neat in the extreme) visited her, he offered to help her clean out and organize her kitchen drawers. Among the clutter, they found $148 in loose change!

Conscious and Subconscious Cures

Usually, feng shui cures affect us subconsciously as well as consciously. A good example is increasing the amount of light in your office in order to stimulate ch'i and prosperity. Good lighting enables you to see clearly so that you can perform tasks more effectively—this is the conscious part of the cure. Subconsciously, light stimulates serotonin production in the brain's hypothalamus, which tends to make you feel more positive and energetic.

The same is true of cures that involve color. Psychological studies have shown that we respond physically to colors, albeit on a subconscious level. When test subjects are seated in a red room, their systems are stimulated. Body temperature, heart rate, and respiration increase, and the subjects tend to overestimate the amount of time they've been in the room. By contrast, people placed in a blue room become more relaxed. Temperature, heart rate, and respiration slow. These subjects usually underestimate the length of time they've been in the blue room.

We also attach psychological significances to colors. Many women like pink, but few men do and they usually consider it to be a "feminine" color. Red is often thought of as a passionate and exciting color, while dark blue is viewed as a sober and serious one. Many of these color connections are cultural. In the West, white is associated with purity; black is linked with mourning. But in China, white is the color of mourning and black is connected with money. Because this book is written for Westerners, I tend to offer feng shui cures in Part Two that draw on Western psychological conditioning and associations. However, I also suggest a number of cures that use Chinese color symbolism, especially red (the color of good luck) and black, because I've found that they work.

Cures involving scents function in a similar manner. As the healing art of aromatherapy has demonstrated, scents affect the limbic system of the brain—the part that's associated with memories and emotions, which is why the aroma of cookies baking can trigger a childhood memory of grandma. Shifts in brain wave activity in response to certain scents can be measured electronically. Because fragrances affect us physically as well as psychologically, they can be powerful when used as feng shui cures.

Cures that act as subconscious motivators are very effective and prevalent in feng shui. These remedies utilize the power of suggestion to focus and strengthen your intention, even if you aren't consciously aware of what's happening. Subconscious motivational devices are often used by people who are trying to lose weight, break bad habits, overcome insomnia, and for lots of other purposes as well. Affirmations—short, positive statements that you repeat often to encourage a desired condition or overcome an unwanted one—are popular subconscious motivators. In Part Two I recommend displaying brief phrases or single words, such as "wealth" or "good luck," in a place where you will see them often in order to impress your objective on the subconscious.

Symbols and pictures can also be powerful motivational tools. As advertising clearly demonstrates, we respond in predictable ways to images that trigger our subconscious minds and emotions. The process of association is what makes these images effective. For example, a company might link a particular drink with fun by showing a picture of a group of friends having a good time while drinking its product. When we see this image, we subconsciously connect the product with happiness and friendship. Feng shui uses pictures that represent desired conditions in much the same way—to trigger your subconscious and motivate it to get you what that picture represents. The more vivid and personal the image is, the better it works.

TYPES OF CURES AND THEIR FUNCTIONS

Feng shui cures act in different ways and are designed to correct different conditions. No single cure will work in every situation. Cures that utilize color or aromas serve as sensory triggers. Cures that involve images or symbolic representations of actual situations function through the process of association. You can't just put any old cure in place and expect it to produce the desired results. A mirror and a wind chime aren't interchangeable options. In fact, using an inappropriate cure may exacerbate a condition or instigate a new set of concerns.

Usually there is more than one solution to a problem and you can choose the one that best suits your taste or needs. The main reason for using any feng shui cure, however, is to establish balance.

Most cures fall into one of the following categories, although some may overlap more than one category.

Unblocking Cures

These cures promote clarity and focus, eliminate obstacles, and enable positive energy to flow smoothly through your home and your life. Simply put, they help you get "unstuck." Unblocking cures include cleaning, organizing, repairing, eliminating clutter, and furniture arranging. They are probably the most common and effective remedies in feng shui's medicine bag. They are also the most logical and "useful" in a practical sense.

Usually it's a good idea to implement unblocking cures first, before trying to get results through other methods. If, for example, you put an activating cure into effect before decluttering your home, you may succeed in stirring up lots of energy, but it won't be able to circulate through your home without bumping into physical obstacles. As a result, you may experience increased stress and confusion.

Activating Cures

These cures stimulate energy and can be used to break up stagnant conditions, prompt change, or redirect the flow of ch'i. Often they use moving objects, such as wind chimes, mobiles, whirligigs, or fans. Electronic equipment and appliances—including computers, stoves, and TVs—stir up sluggish ch'i, too. Music and sounds such as those produced by bells, wind chimes, and singing bowls, also fall into this category. Moving furniture or objects around in your home has an activating effect—even physically walking through the rooms of your home stirs up energy patterns and encourages movement in the various areas of your life. Straight lines, which conduct ch'i from one point to another along the most direct route, can also serve as activating cures.

STABILIZING CURES

The opposite of activating cures, these remedies are used to slow down or concentrate ch'i. When energy moves too quickly through your home, it can produce sudden changes, instability, and stress. This "rushing" ch'i, as rapidly flowing vital energy is called, doesn't have time to nourish you or your home properly, so relationships, finances, and other areas of your life may suffer. Stabilizing cures "hold down" ch'i, and include heavy statuary, rocks, large pieces of furniture, and other objects that have mass and weight. Square shapes, which we associate with stability (because squares are hard to push over), fall into this category, too.

AUGMENTING CURES

When more is considered better, these are the best cures to use. Augmenting cures promote growth and increase. Live plants, which grow and thereby symbolize expansion, are the most popular augmenting cure. Wood comes from trees, so by extension anything made of wood falls into this category.

In some situations, mirrors can be used to encourage growth. For example, mirroring a wall in a small room gives the impression that the room is much larger. When a mirror is hung so that it reflects an object, the mirror "doubles" it so that it seems as if there are two objects instead of one.

Ten Common Feng Shui Cures

Feng shui cures are designed to increase, disperse, modulate, or otherwise alter the movement of ch'i through a particular space. In theory, the number of possible cures is probably endless, and as you become familiar with feng shui you'll undoubtedly come up with ideas of your own. The following remedies, however, are commonly used in the practice of feng shui. One (or a combination) of them will effectively resolve nearly any problem in nearly any environment.

Light: Electric lights function as artificial sunshine. By simply turning on a light, we can "extend" daylight. Dimmer switches allow us to control the amount of light we shine into our living and work spaces. Lights of all kinds (including candles, lanterns, and gas lamps as well as electric lights) augment the fire element and the yang force. Crystals and light-catchers also fall into this category because they catch, reflect, and enhance sunlight, thereby augmenting its power.

One of the most frequently utilized feng shui cures, light is used to bring warmth (either physically or psychologically) into a cold or dark room, to stimulate or activate sluggish ch'i, to increase the amount of vital energy in a particular area, or to fill in a missing sector in an irregularly shaped space.

Mirrors: Mirrors can be used in a variety of ways: to open up a confining space, to augment ch'i or direct its movement, or to increase the power of a symbol. The reflecting nature of mirrors lets you position them to deflect unwanted energies or to attract and enhance desirable energies.

For instance, you could hang a mirror on an exterior door to "bounce" disturbing energy caused by traffic or street noise back to the source and away from your home. Mirrors can also be used to create the illusion of space and openness. Hung on a wall in a small room, they reflect the opposite wall and seemingly double the space. When hung on a slanting ceiling or enclosing wall, a mirror serves as a symbolic window. To double the influence of an object, hang a mirror so that the object is reflected and visually "cloned."

Living Things: Because feng shui seeks to improve our connection with the natural world and the Tao, its practitioners often bring nature indoors in the forms of plants, fish, birds, and water fountains. Living things symbolize growth, so cures that utilize them generally promote increase and expansion. Plants provide an additional benefit, too—they absorb carbon dioxide in the air and help us to breathe better. Water nurtures all life, so cures that involve water, such as fountains, bird baths, and aquariums, are used symbolically to attract or strengthen the life-giving power of ch'i. (Notice how many Chinese restaurants feature aquariums in their decor.)

Moving Objects: Moving objects stir up and activate ch'i, to keep it from getting "stuck." Wind chimes, mobiles, fans, fountains, and whirligigs are popular cures of this type. These remedies can also be used indoors or outside to direct the flow of ch'i or to deflect unwanted energy away from your home.

Heavy Objects: Heavy objects provide stability by "holding down" ch'i so it doesn't move through a space too rapidly. Large stones, statuary, heavy pieces of furniture, large plants, and other objects that have weight and mass fall into this category. These cures are beneficial for stabilizing unsettled situations or when you want to hold onto something that seems to be slipping away. They can also be used to concentrate energy in a particular area.

Sound: Pleasing sounds can improve the energy patterns in your environment. Soothing music promotes feelings of peace and harmony among the home's occupants. Lively music awakens sluggish ch'i and can provide balance in an area that has too much yin energy. Wind chimes, bells, and singing bowls are frequently used in feng shui to activate stuck ch'i, disperse or reroute disruptive ch'i, and summon positive ch'i.

Electrical Objects: Electrical objects—stereos, televisions, computers, air conditioners, stoves, and other appliances—stimulate ch'i and keep it from stagnating. These items promote movement, activity, and change. They can also be used to balance an area that contains too much of the yin force.

Colors: Colors affect us physically and psychologically. In feng shui, the symbolism inherent in colors as well as their influence on us can be used to cure certain problems. These are discussed in greater depth later.

Scents: As discussed earlier, scents affect us in subtle and profound ways, both consciously and unconsciously. Incense, potpourri, scented candles, essential oils, perfume, and other fragrant items are effective and versatile feng shui cures.

Although personal preferences must be taken into account, the art of aromatherapy has shown that certain scents influence us in measurable and distinct ways. Pine, peppermint, and eucalyptus are stimulating and help to promote mental clarity. Vanilla, lavender, and chamomile have a calming effect on us. Amber, cinnamon, and cedar encourage sensations of warmth; citrus and mint fragrances tend to make us feel cooler. Sage has long been used in many cultures to purify and clear the air. Rose, ylang-ylang, musk, patchouli, bergamot, and jasmine are known for their aphrodisiac qualities.

Images: Pictures, symbols, icons, sculpture, and other images trigger subconscious associations for us and serve as psychological motivators. They can be used as powerful feng shui cures to encourage certain associations, strengthen intentions, or prompt emotional responses. For example, a picture of a happy couple makes us think of love and companionship. A trophy connotes success. A Rolls Royce is an obvious symbol of wealth.

Feng Shui Symbolism

More than just a convenient form of graphic shorthand, symbols contain within their patterns the essence of the things they represent. Some symbols are universal. These appear in cultures around the world, both ancient and modern. People everywhere respond to these symbols in pretty much the same way. For example, the egg has long been associated with birth and fertility. Other symbols are personal and have significance for you alone. Both personal and collective symbols can be tapped in feng shui to produce results. Colors, numbers, logos, and geometric shapes are some familiar symbols that we see and use daily, usually without giving it a second thought.

When you view a meaningful symbol, an instant recognition is sparked at a very deep, subconscious level—even if you don't consciously understand the symbol's meaning. Your response to the symbol may cause you to act in a certain way. Because symbols influence us subliminally, they can be very powerful tools for producing results. In feng shui, you can intentionally choose symbols that will generate particular responses in order to bring about the conditions you want in your life.

In Part Two, I recommend using many different types of symbols, including hexagram patterns from the *I Ching* (an ancient Chinese oracle), astrological glyphs, and other easily identifiable symbols such as geometric shapes. If you wish, you can "mix and match" symbols to create unique and very specific cures.

Color

Color enriches every area of our lives, aesthetically, psychologically, and physically. Following are some basic color associations that you can use in feng shui cures to bring about desired conditions in every area of your life.

Red: Considered to be a lucky color, red is associated with the fire element, strength, activity, and passion. In China, it is believed to bring happiness, good fortune, and fame. Chinese brides typically wear red. Gifts of money are given in red envelopes. Many feng shui cures use red ribbons, red envelopes, or red ink for calligraphy. Red attracts positive energy and dispels bad luck.

Orange: A blend of red and yellow, orange (and its variations peach, coral, and russet) contains some characteristics of both of these other hues. It stimulates ch'i and symbolizes happiness and power.

Yellow/Gold: In China, palaces were painted yellow because this was considered to be the color of authority. In the West, yellow is representative of the sun and its life-giving warmth. Psychologically, yellow encourages feelings of optimism and cheerfulness.

Green: The color of plants, green is associated with growth. A calming color, it also has a relaxing influence on us.

Blue: The color of water and the sky, blue reminds us of nature and conveys a sense of serenity. Its soothing influence can help to counteract stress or hyperactivity. We associate light blue with hope and purity, dark blue with seriousness and dignity.

Purple: In many cultures purple has been considered a "royal" color, reserved for the wealthy and powerful. In some Western religions, it is linked with spirituality and worn by religious leaders. In China, purple is thought to be a fortunate color—some say even luckier than red.

Pink: Pink is associated with love, affection, and joy. Psychological studies show that this color produces feelings of sociability and congeniality.

Black: Black is the color of money in China. In the West, it is associated with seriousness, formality, and wisdom. A blend of all colors of the spectrum, black can be used in feng shui to increase mental activity and communication.

Brown: We connect brown with the earth, trees, and stones; therefore, this color symbolizes stability and permanence.

COLOR AND THE FIVE ELEMENTS

Fire = Red, orange

Water = Black, dark blue

Earth = Yellow, brown

Wood = Green, blue

Metal = White, gray

Shapes

Our environments are comprised of shapes—natural and manmade. Some manmade structures are intentionally fashioned to imitate natural ones. The pyramids, for example, simulate mountains; swimming pools represent ponds.

We respond to these shapes with the subconscious, just as we respond to colors. Artists often incorporate carefully chosen shapes into their work to convey certain concepts. *I Ching* coins combine two basic symbols: a circle (representing heaven) with a square (representing earth) cut out of the center.

In feng shui, we can tap the deeper meanings inherent in shapes to create the circumstances we desire. In Part Two, I offer a number of cures that use shapes to produce effects. The following list briefly explains the significances, in feng shui terms, of some familiar geometric shapes.

Shapes and Their Meanings

Circle = wholeness, continuity, unity, harmony, heaven

Square = solidity, permanence, stability, earth

Triangle = movement, change, direction toward a goal

Rectangle = growth, expansion

Curved or wavy lines = flexibility, interaction, adaptability

Straight lines = rapid movement, one-pointedness

NUMBERS

Usually, we think of numbers as units of measurement. However, numbers contain hidden, mystical meanings as well. The study of numerology connects each letter of the alphabet with a number. Each number has a unique energy vibration, and these vibrations can be utilized in feng shui as cures. As you may have noticed, shapes and numbers overlap—because their vibrations are similar, you can use either one to produce the same result. The following list briefly describes the meaning of each number.

Numbers and Their Meanings

0 = unity, wholeness, harmony, continuity

1 = beginnings, the individual

2 = polarity, pairing, complementary forces

3 = creativity, growth, movement toward a goal

4 = stability, permanence

5 = change, activity, instability

6 = cooperation, give-and-take

7 = withdrawal, introspection

8 = money, business, material power

9 = fulfillment, completion

CURES YOU CAN DO IN 10 MINUTES OR LESS

THE EASY, INEXPENSIVE CURES in this

chapter can be implemented quickly—usually in ten minutes or less—and require no special knowledge, skills, or tools. But despite their simplicity, they are very effective and should begin working almost immediately. Allow the results a little time to manifest, however, especially if the condition you are attempting to correct has been in existence for quite a while.

The cures are grouped into four categories: Prosperity, Love, Good Luck and Happiness, and Health/Well-Being. Many of the cures work best if they are applied in the rooms that relate to the area of life you wish to influence, as discussed in chapter 2. I briefly explain the feng shui philosophy and symbolism behind each cure to help you understand why these tried-and-true techniques work. The explanations also describe which conditions the cures are designed to remedy—some cures are more suitable for certain situations than others.

As I've stated before, you don't have to understand or believe in the esoteric dimensions of feng shui in order to reap the benefits. However, because your intent is a key component in feng shui's effectiveness, I suggest you implement these cures with sincerity and have confidence that they will work. Your attitude and expectations can influence the outcome. In feng shui, as in other types of problem solving, if you approach the challenge half-heartedly or doubt that you will succeed, you are likely to get less-than-satisfactory results.

I recommend that you try a few cures at first, then wait a week or so before making any other changes. During this time, observe the large and subtle shifts in your life, particularly in the areas you've focused on. Interestingly, you may notice that although you've implemented cures to enhance your financial situation, after putting feng shui into practice, your health improves, too. This happens because feng shui balances all facets of your life and restores harmony on every level.

If you don't feel that the cures you've performed are working quickly enough, try a few more. Again, it's a good idea to wait a couple of weeks to see what transpires before enacting any additional remedies. Remember, you are putting potentially powerful changes into motion, and change—even when it's positive—can be stressful, so go slow.

PROSPERITY

Turn on your stove for at least ten minutes every day.

The Chinese believe that the stove generates prosperity, because this is where we prepare meals to nourish ourselves and our loved ones. But to take advantage of the stove's wealth-producing potential, you must use it—even if you only light a burner to make a cup of tea.

Hang a mirror above your stove.

A mirror reflects the stovetop and effectively "doubles" your stove's wealth-producing capabilities.

Hang a mirror beside your stove.

Use this cure if your stove is positioned in a corner, against a wall, so that you feel cramped while cooking. This situation can constrict your earning ability. To alleviate it, hang a mirror on the side wall to create the illusion of space.

Place a bowl or jar near your front door and drop a penny in it each time you go in or out.

Ch'i enters your home through the front door. Because positive ch'i enhances whatever it touches, it stimulates financial growth when it encounters the coins. From a psychological perspective, each time you drop a coin in the bowl, you reaffirm your intention to become more prosperous.

Fill a jar with pennies and bury it outside your kitchen.
When you do this cure you are planting "seed money"
that will grow steadily in time.

**Clear the passageways to and through
your home office or work area.**
When your workplace is free of obstructions, you—and ch'i—
can move through the space easily and function more effectively,
so your ability to generate wealth is enhanced.

Replace a washer in a leaky kitchen faucet.

A dripping faucet in the kitchen, where wealth is generated,
can cause money to slowly leak away.

Mend a hole in a pocket.

This cure has powerful, symbolic qualities—and practical ones, as
well. To keep money from slipping away, mend a hole in your pocket.

**Put three coins in a red envelope
and place it on your computer or desk.**

Red is considered a lucky color in China and three is a lucky number.
This simple ritual combines both symbols of good luck to attract money.

**Fill a small red envelope with rice and
place it on a shelf in your kitchen.**

Rice is a staple food in China and a symbol of prosperity. Red is a
lucky color, so this combination encourages financial good luck.

**Tie three *I Ching* coins together with a red ribbon
and hang them above your stove.**

These coins, which have square holes in the center, are lucky talismans—especially when tied together with a lucky red ribbon. Three is considered a fortunate number in China and is the number of growth. Hanging the coins above your stove increases its wealth-generating possibilities.

**Tie three *I Ching* coins together with a red ribbon
and hang them from a tree in your front yard.**

This cure combines several lucky symbols—coins, the number three, red, and wood—to attract and increase your prosperity.

Tie eight *I Ching* coins together with a red ribbon
and hang them near your computer, desk, or workstation.
Eight is the number of financial success and stability—goals that are
enhanced by the symbolism of the coins and the lucky red ribbon.

Display a gold star in your work area.
Remember when teachers gave gold stars to students for doing
excellent work? This cure uses the same symbolism to encourage you
to do your best and to succeed financially and professionally.

**Hang a wind chime in a window
directly across from your front door.**

If a window is in direct line with your front door, ch'i will enter your
home and rush out immediately, taking your money with it.
Hang a wind chime in the window to circulate ch'i through
your home and bring you prosperity.

Put a live plant in your workplace or kitchen.

Plants symbolize growth and new life. By putting a plant in your
workplace, you encourage career success and financial growth.
For best results, pot a plant with round leaves in a shiny golden,
silver, or copper container (the metals from which coins are made).

Place a large plant near the back door.

Use this cure if your front door and back door are in direct line to each other, at either end of a hallway, for instance. In a design like this, ch'i enters your home through the front door and rushes straight out the back door, taking your money with it. The plant prevents money from going out as quickly as it comes in.

Pot a plant in a red container.

To stimulate your income, pot the plant in a container that is red (the color of good luck).

Pot plants in earthenware or ceramic containers.
Use this cure if money passes through your hands too quickly.
Terra cotta, ceramic, and pottery containers represent the
earth element and help to secure your finances.

Tape three coins underneath a plant.
The plant symbolizes growth, so by affixing coins to a flowerpot
that contains a living plant, you encourage financial growth.

**Place a dried "money plant" in a vase and
set it on your desk or workstation.**

When the seedpods of the money plant dry in the autumn,
they resemble silver dollars. Arrange a bunch of these pretty, silvery
stalks in a vase and set them in your work area, where they will
remind you of your goal to attract money.

Replace low-wattage light bulbs in your kitchen with brighter ones.

Brighter lights not only enable you to see better when you're
working but also stimulate positive ch'i and prosperity.
(Note: Incandescent or full-spectrum lights are generally easier
on the eyes than fluorescent bulbs.)

Vacuum or dust the lampshades in your office or work area.
Dirty shades dim the amount of light generated by your lamps,
so keep them clean to allow ch'i to brighten your financial picture.

Set a large stone just inside your back door.
This cure is good for people who have trouble holding on to money.
Heavy objects help "hold down" ch'i so it doesn't leave your home too
rapidly, taking your prosperity with it.

Set two large stones at the bottom of a steep flight of steps.
A long, steep stairway leading to your front door can cause ch'i
and money to roll away from your home. Place two large stones at
the bottom of the stairway, one at each side, to hold onto ch'i
and keep it from slipping away.

**Hang a mirror above your desk so that when you are seated,
the entrance to your work area is reflected in the mirror.**
Use this alternate cure if you cannot place your desk in a spot that
makes it easy for you to see the entrance to your work area.
This allows you to easily see anyone who may enter your work space,
without having to turn around.

Hang an octagonal mirror above your computer.

Eight is the number of business and finance. In China, the octagon is considered to be an auspicious shape. A mirror placed to reflect your computer symbolically "doubles" its wealth-generating capabilities. Use a bagua mirror (available in Chinese gift shops and places where feng shui supplies are sold) for best results.

Mirror a "missing corner" in your office or kitchen.

If your office or kitchen is irregularly shaped and has a notched out corner or section that appears to be "missing," you may be missing out on financial benefits or opportunities. Hang mirrors on the walls of the missing corner to cut symbolic "windows" in these walls and open them up so they don't limit your wealth.

**Combine the colors red, yellow, white, black,
and green in your office or work area.**

These colors correspond to the five elements. Including them
all in your work space establishes balance and can help you
improve your earning ability.

Create a balance of all five elements in your kitchen.

In a glass jar or container, place a wooden spoon, a knife, a long
fireplace match or lighter, and a ceramic cooking implement. This
cure combines articles that represent all five Chinese elements to
establish balance in your kitchen and encourage prosperity.

Hang a small, faceted crystal ball or
set a piece of clear quartz crystal at a kitchen window.
Crystals reflect light and boost its money-generating potential.
This cure is especially good to use in small kitchens that don't
receive much natural light or that aren't used very often.

Hang a small, faceted crystal ball or set a clear quartz crystal
at a window of your home office or work space.
Crystals catch and augment natural light, boosting its power and
potential. The more light you shine into your work area, the more
positive energy you have available to focus on improving your finances.

Illuminate dark corners in your office or work area.

A dark corner in your office or work space saps positive ch'i and diminishes its power to produce wealth. Position a lamp so it shines light into a dark corner.

Illuminate dark corners in your kitchen.

Hang a small, faceted crystal ball or other light catcher from the ceiling in a shadowy corner to reflect light into the darkness. For best results, hang the crystal from a piece of red cord that's nine inches long (nine is the number of fulfillment and red is considered a lucky "fire" color).

Place a vase of yellow flowers in your kitchen.

Flowers symbolize the stage of blossoming and fulfillment in the life cycle; therefore, they encourage prosperity when placed in your kitchen. Yellow—the color of the sun and gold— reminds you of your goal to increase your wealth.

For best results, put the flowers in a green vase.

Place a vase of yellow and red flowers in your office or work area.

This cure combines two fortunate colors—red and yellow—to stimulate financial growth. Replace the flowers when they start to wilt.

**Place a black stone—such as onyx, tourmaline,
or obsidian—in your office or work area.**

Black is the color of money in China. Stones "hold down" money
and keep it from slipping away too quickly. These black gemstones, in particular, contain subtle energies that can help solidify
your financial situation and provide greater security.

Place a piece of amethyst on your desk or computer.

This gemstone is known for its calming properties, so placing one in
your office can help you cope with stress or tight deadlines.

Put an egg-shaped object in your office.
This cure helps you attract new business or new money-making
opportunities, because eggs symbolize birth and fertility.
For best results, choose an egg made of jade or aventurine—
stones that are associated with prosperity.

Place a quartz crystal on your computer or beside your phone.
Quartz crystals enhance whatever they contact,
so putting a chunk of clear quartz crystal on your computer
can augment your earning capacity and putting one
on your phone can open lines of communication.

Carry a crystal in your purse.

Because crystals augment whatever they touch,
this cure helps to expand your finances.

Carry a crystal in your briefcase.

This cure is similar to the above one. In this case, the crystal helps
you attract new business and increase your earning potential.

Carry money in a black wallet or purse.

Black is the color of money in China, so this cure helps
to improve your financial situation.

Carry money in a white or gray wallet or purse.

White and gray are colors feng shui associates with the metal element, which represents stability and permanence. This cure helps you hold onto money.

Frame a paper money bill and display it prominently in your office or work space.

Each time you look at this obvious symbol of wealth, you will be reminded of your goal to attract money.

For best results, choose a golden-colored frame.

**Frame a paper money bill and display it
prominently in your kitchen.**

Like the previous cure, this one works through the power of
suggestion. For best results, hang the framed bill near your stove
where it will remind you of your intention to be more prosperous.

Tie a red ribbon around a piggy bank or cash box.

Red is considered to be a lucky color and can enhance the imagery of
a piggy bank or cash box, thereby drawing more money to you.

Tie a red ribbon around paid bills, then file them away.
When you perform this simple ritual, you eliminate any bad feelings
you may have about paying bills and demonstrate confidence that you
will always be able to take care of all your bills promptly.

Close toilet lids.
Ch'i flows away from your home via drains, especially the toilet.
Closing the toilet lid keeps money from "going down the drain."

Set a live plant on the tank of your toilet.
The plant draws ch'i upward, away from the toilet, keeping it—
and your money—from being flushed away.

Close the bathroom door and the shower curtain.
By keeping these closed, you prevent ch'i—
and prosperity—from slipping away down the drain.

Hang a small, faceted crystal ball from the ceiling,
just outside your bathroom.
This cure draws ch'i up and away from the bathroom and keeps
money from going down the drain.

Hang a wind chime between the bathroom's entrance and the toilet.
This cure circulates ch'i away from the toilet and
keeps your wealth from being flushed away.

**If a bathroom is next to your kitchen, hang a
wind chime from the ceiling outside of the bathroom door.**
This circulates the positive ch'i that's generated in your kitchen away
from the bathroom and into other parts of your home, thereby
preventing ch'i—and your money—from disappearing down the drain.

**If a bathroom is next to your office or work space, hang
a small mirror on the outside of the bathroom door.**
This deflects the positive ch'i that's generated in your office
away from the bathroom and prevents it—and your money—
from disappearing down the drain.

Move your desk if it shares a wall with the toilet.

If your desk is on the same wall as the toilet—even if they are on opposite sides of the wall—move the desk to another location. This prevents money from going down the drain.

Hang an attractive picture on the wall above the toilet.

This focuses your attention away from the toilet and keeps ch'i from being flushed away.

Hang a mobile in your kitchen.

This cure is especially useful if your finances have been stagnant for a while. Moving objects stir up ch'i and help stimulate prosperity.

**Hang a wooden wind chime
in the window of your office or work space.**
Like the previous cure, the wind chime's movement activates stagnant ch'i and stimulates your money-making potential. The chime's pleasant sound provides additional benefits, too: It soothes you and reminds you of your goal to attract prosperity each time you hear it ring. Wood is a symbol of growth.

**Hang a glass wind chime in the window
of your office or work space.**
Glass facilitates mental activity and communication, so this is good for people who work in communications fields, computers, or sales.

Place a small fountain in your office or work area.

The soothing effect of running water helps reduce tension in your workplace, while providing symbolic nourishment to increase your income. The stones in the fountain help stabilize your finances so you don't spend more as you earn more.

Hang a picture of trees, flowers, or other plants in your kitchen.

Plants suggest growth, so hanging an attractive picture of trees or flowers in your kitchen provides a pleasing focal point while also encouraging financial growth. For best results, frame your picture in a golden or silvery frame.

**Hang a picture of a landscape
with a distant view in your dining room.**

This cure is good to use in a small dining room or one that doesn't
have a window. The picture symbolically opens up the enclosed,
claustrophobic space and expands your financial opportunities.

Hang a rectangular mirror in your dining room.

Here's another cure for a small or windowless dining room.
The mirror creates an illusion of space and expands the room—
and your money-making ability. For best results, the mirror should
be rectangular because this shape symbolizes growth.

**On your kitchen windowsill or in your office,
set three objects that signify wealth.**

Three is the number of action, motivation, and change. It also suggests putting ideas into motion. Choose three items that symbolize riches to encourage action toward increasing your wealth.

Arrange objects in a triangular pattern for best results.

**Place four objects that symbolize wealth in a pottery bowl
and set them on your kitchen counter.**

Use this cure if money tends to burn a hole in your pocket. Four is the number of stability, so arrange the objects in a square pattern for best results. The earth element, represented by the pottery bowl, also helps you hold onto money.

Display the symbol "Ta Yu" in a prominent spot in your kitchen or work area.

This symbol from the *I Ching*, an ancient Chinese oracle, means "Possession in Great Measure." Its significance will be imprinted on your subconscious each time you look at it, thereby reminding you of your goal to become more prosperous.

Draw the symbol for the planet Jupiter on a piece of paper
and display it in a place where you'll see it often.
Jupiter, the largest planet in our solar system, is considered to be the
astrological representative of abundance. This planet's symbol helps
expand your wealth and bring good fortune.

**Position the breadwinner's dining chair so that
this person faces the entrance to the room when seated.**
Considered the place of honor in China, this seating arrangement
gives the "best seat in the house" to the person whose income you
wish to augment. If you want to increase someone else's money-
making ability, position that person's chair in this auspicious spot.

Place four chairs around your kitchen or dining table.
This cure is good for people who have trouble holding on to money.
Because four is the number of stability, this cure helps you
to stabilize your finances and save money.

Burn three candles on your kitchen or dining table.

Three is a number of growth and change. Candles represent the fire element and enhance ch'i. This cure combines both symbols to stimulate prosperity. For best results, use green or black candles.

Use a green tablecloth on your kitchen or dining table.

Green is the color of plants, so it suggests growth. It is also the color of paper money in some countries. When you eat meals from a table draped in green, you "nourish" yourself with these images of prosperity.

Use a yellow tablecloth on your kitchen or dining table.
Yellow represents gold as well as the sun's life-giving rays.
When you eat meals from a table draped in golden yellow, you
"nourish" yourself with these images.

Hang herbs and flowers on an exposed beam in your kitchen.
Heavy beams—especially if they are positioned above your stove—
symbolically depress ch'i and limit your stove's wealth-producing
potential. To soften the weighty influence of an exposed beam, hang
fresh or dried herbs or flowers on it.

Don't place your desk under an exposed beam.

Heavy beams compress ch'i. If your desk or workstation is positioned under an exposed beam, its depressing influence can hold down your ability to earn money. Move your desk to another location.

Attach red ribbon or fringe to an exposed beam in your office.

If you can't move your desk, this cure uses the fiery energy of red (a lucky color in China) to diminish the depressing influence of a heavy beam, so it doesn't limit your earning ability.

Hang a small mirror on a slanting ceiling or eaves in your office.

A slanted ceiling or eaves in your office "hold down" ch'i, limiting its positive energy and wealth-producing capability. This is especially problematic if your desk or computer is positioned beneath the slant. Hang a small mirror on the slanted ceiling to "open up" its depressing influence. The mirror also reflects the image of your computer or desk and "doubles" its income-producing potential.

Position a mirror to reflect a body of water.

This cure is for people who live near a body of water—a lake, the ocean, a river, or a stream. Water, which nourishes all life, can also symbolically nourish your finances and help increase your income. Hang a mirror so that it reflects the view of water and "draws" its wealth-producing energy to you.

Burn incense in a bamboo holder.

Incense is often used symbolically to carry requests to the heavens.
Bamboo is considered a symbol of good fortune in China, so by
combining a fire cure (burning incense) with wood
(signifying growth) you stimulate prosperity.

Burn incense in a ceramic holder.

Earthenware or porcelain incense holders help stabilize
your finances, so money doesn't go out as quickly as it comes in.

Burn pine incense in your work space.

The study of aromatherapy shows that scents affect the brain.
The scent of pine helps to clear your mind so you can focus better.
Pine is also symbolic of financial stability, because pine trees
remain green even in the winter.

Burn mint incense in your kitchen.

Mint is another symbol of prosperity, so burning mint-scented
incense helps draw money to you. The study of aromatherapy
shows that scenting your kitchen with mint has another benefit,
too—it sparks your appetite.

**Tie eight small bells on a red cord
and hang them on the door to your office or work area.**
Each time you open your door, the ringing bells remind
you of your intention to attract wealth. Eight is the number of
business and finance. The bells also prevent you from being
distracted while you work, because they will ring to alert
you if anyone enters your work space.

**Place three coins in a wooden box
and set it in your office or work area.**
The wood element is connected with growth and so is the number
three. This cure combines both symbols to increase prosperity.

**In your office, hang a picture of a landscape
with a mountain in the distance.**

Visual images influence you at a subconscious level. The mountain represents your long-term financial goals, still in the distance, and the heights to which you aspire. When you look at this picture, you are encouraged to continue striving for greater achievements and rewards. For best results, frame the picture in a wooden frame.

Place a figurine of a lion in your office or kitchen.

The lion is the king of beasts and a symbol of royalty. Set a small sculpture of a lion on your desk or on your countertop, where it will provide a positive image for you and help you attract wealth and power. If possible, find a small figurine of a lion sculpted in jade.

Set a small piece of jade on a kitchen windowsill.
Jade is considered a stone of good fortune in China—and its green color symbolizes paper money in some countries. Place it on a kitchen windowsill to attract wealth.

Set eight pieces of jade on your computer, desk, or work station.
The lucky vibrations in jade can also help you attract prosperity when the stone is placed in your office or work space. Eight is the number of business and finance, so you increase your earning potential by placing eight pieces of jade where you will see them often.

Set a small pyramid or obelisk on your desk or computer.
Upward-pointing triangles signify growth and movement toward the
top. A prominently placed pyramid or obelisk can help you raise your
sights and increase your income. (Try to find one made of jade.)

Use black accents or accessories in your office.
The color of money in China, black can be beneficial when
used in small amounts in your work area. It also facilitates
communication with business associates and clients.

Display an upward-pointing red triangle in your office or work area.
This fire cure stimulates activity and change in your financial situation. Red is a lucky color. The triangle's upward point suggests growth and encourages you to set your sights high.

Display a green square in your office or work area.
Use this earth cure if your goal is to save money and create a more stable financial situation. Green is the color of plants—which symbolize growth—and of paper money in some countries. The square is an inherently solid geometric shape.

Place a wooden bowl or other open,
wooden container on your kitchen counter.

Wood cures encourage growth and expansion.

An open bowl or container suggests that you are

psychologically open to receiving and collecting abundance.

Display the number 1 in your office
to spark a new business venture or idea.

One is the number of beginnings and can inspire you

to initiate new money-making goals, projects, or ideas.

Display the number 8 to stabilize finances.
Eight is the number of business and financial stability, so it can help you hold onto money or find ways to build slowly and steadily toward your financial goals.

Above your computer or desk,
hang a crystal on a nine-inch-long red cord.
This cure combines two lucky symbols—the number nine, which signifies fulfillment, and the color red—to increase your earning power.

Place eight stones in a wooden box and set it in your kitchen.
This cure helps you save money and make practical
financial decisions. It combines the growth-producing aspects
of wood with the stabilizing energy of stones and the number eight.

Organize your desk so that file folders,
correspondence, and other materials that relate to new projects
or financial ventures are positioned in the eastern section.
The east, where the sun rises, is considered the point of new
beginnings, so this is a good spot to keep your "new business" paperwork.

Create a focal point in your office or work space.

When your mind starts to wander, use this focal point to bring your attention back to your objective: to earn money. A focal point should be something attractive—a picture, a vase of flowers, an attractive or meaningful item—and ideally should include the colors red (for luck) and white (to enhance concentration).

Chant a prosperity affirmation three times upon entering your office or work space.

Chanting is a common practice among Buddhists as a way of reinforcing an intention and causing a desired condition to manifest. Repeat a short phrase, such as "My life is rich in every way," three times each day when you first enter your office or workplace.

— LOVE —

**Clear away any clutter or obstacles near
the entrance to your bedroom.**
This enables ch'i to enter your bedroom easily and
invites love to come into your life, unobstructed.

Clear the passageways through your bedroom.
This enables you—and ch'i—to move easily through your bedroom
and invites romance to flow smoothly into your life.

Dust the furniture in your bedroom.
Remove dust and cobwebs, which signify disuse
or neglect, to activate your love life.

Vacuum or dust the lampshades in your bedroom.
Dirty shades dim the amount of light generated by your lamps,
so keep them clean to allow ch'i to brighten your love life.

Clean under the bed.
This cure helps you clear away obstacles and problems—especially
unspoken grudges or resentments—from your relationship.

Don't let clutter accumulate on your night stand.

Clutter distracts and causes confusion, so keep your night stand neat to avoid confusion in your love life.

Wash a window in your bedroom.

Ch'i enters your home through the windows of your home. Make sure your bedroom windows are clean to allow as much positive ch'i—and love—into your life as possible.

Replace a burned-out light bulb in your bedroom.

Nonfunctioning items represent areas of your life that aren't working out. Light, in particular, increases positive ch'i, so this fire cure keeps romance from burning out in your life.

Hang a wooden wind chime in your bedroom window.
Wind chimes activate ch'i and keep it from stagnating. Hang a
wooden one in your bedroom to attract new love and stir up
excitement in your love life.

Hang a glass wind chime in your bedroom window.
This cure improves communication between you and a partner
and encourages compromise.

Replace flowers as soon as they start to fade.
Flowers that are past their prime symbolize withering
and death, so remove them as soon as they start
to fade and replace them with fresh ones.

Put red or pink sheets on your bed.

The colors of passion and affection,

red and pink stimulate loving feelings.

Place a portable electric fan in your bedroom.

Fans stir up "stuck" ch'i and keep your love life from growing stale.

Smudge your bedroom.

Smudging gets rid of bad vibes that may be interfering with your

love life. This cleansing ritual is especially good if you have ended one

relationship and want to begin a new one. It can also "clear the air"

between you and a partner. Burn bundled sage or sage incense in your

bedroom to purify the space and remove emotional blockage.

Put a live plant in your bedroom.

Plants represent growth and life, so placing one in your bedroom can encourage growth in romantic areas. For best results, choose a plant with pink or red flowers or one with rounded leaves.

Remove a plant with spiky leaves or points.

Cacti and other plants with pointed leaves can spark prickly conditions between you and a partner. (Roses are the exception.)

Pot a plant in a red container.

Red is a lucky color and also one that suggests passion,
so pot a plant in a red container to enliven your love life.

Pot a plant in a ceramic or earthenware container.

This earth cure encourages stability and security in a relationship.

**Hang a small, faceted crystal ball from your bedroom
ceiling on a red, nine-inch-long cord or ribbon.**

This cure lights up your love life. A crystal ball catches and
reflects light, so it brightens the area where you hang it.
Red is a lucky color in China, and nine is the number of fulfillment.

Burn sensual or exotic incense in your bedroom.

Your emotions are affected by aromas. Scents such as jasmine, rose, ylang-ylang, and musk stimulate feelings of love and desire.

Burn incense in a wooden holder.

Wood symbolizes growth, so using a wooden incense holder—especially one made of bamboo—helps you attract a partner and increases your love.

Burn incense in a ceramic holder.

This earth cure encourages comfort and security in a relationship.

Dab on a small amount of perfume each night before going to sleep.
Perfume has long been considered an aphrodisiac, and wearing it makes you feel desirable. Jasmine, rose, ylang-ylang, musk, or patchouli are some scents to consider because they are linked with love and passion.

Put a scented sachet in your underwear drawer.
Like the above cure, this one uses aromatherapy as well as the power of suggestion to spark passion in your love life. Choose a scent that's associated with love, such as rose or jasmine.

Hang three pictures in a triangular arrangement in your bedroom.
This cure uses the number three to stimulate activity and
excitement in your love life. (Make sure the pictures you
choose convey appropriate symbolism.)

Hang four pictures in a square configuration in your bedroom.
This cure uses the number four to promote trust, security, and stability
in a relationship. (Choose pictures that convey your intention.)

Choose rectangular, wooden frames for pictures.
This cure uses the wood element to promote growth in an existing
relationship or to help you attract new love into your life.

**Draw two black wavy lines on a piece of
paper and place it in your nightstand.**
Wavy lines and the color black are symbols of communication.
This cure helps improve communication between you and
a romantic partner.

Rearrange the objects on your dresser.
This cure keeps your love life from stagnating and encourages
you to stay open to change, new experiences, and excitement.

Tie two bells together with a red ribbon
and hang them on your bedroom doorknob.
This cure makes lovely music each time you open your bedroom door
and reminds you of your intention to draw more love into your life.
It also helps you relax while you are in bed because the bells
will alert you if anyone enters the room.

Position your bed so that when you
are in it you can easily see the entrance to the room.
This keeps you from being distracted or uneasy when you are in bed,
because you are able to see anyone who might enter the room.

Hang a mirror so you can see the entrance to the room reflected in the mirror while you are in bed.
Use this cure if you cannot position your bed so that it's easy to see the door. In this case, the mirror allows you to see anyone who enters the room.

Move your bed if it shares the same wall as a toilet.
If your bed is on the same wall as the toilet—even if they are on opposite sides of the wall—you may find that feelings of affection between you and a partner disappear quickly. Move the bed to another location.

Burn two red candles in your bedroom.

Candles create a romantic mood and red is the color of passion,
so this combination stimulates romantic feelings.

Burn two pink candles in your bedroom.

If you are seeking affection rather than passion,
burn pink candles instead of red ones.

Burn candles in brass or silver candlesticks.

Metal candlesticks promote fidelity, devotion, and stability in a
relationship. Use silver to strengthen a woman's commitment, use
brass to strengthen a man's.

Place two pink or red throw pillows on your bed.
This cure combines two symbols of love—the number
two and the color red or pink—to attract romance.

Place a round, wooden bowl or open container in your bedroom.
The wood element is associated with growth and increase.
Circles signify harmony and unity. An open container shows
you are open to receiving love. Together, these three symbols
form a powerful love cure.

**Write the word "love" on a piece of paper with a
red pen, then place the paper in a wooden box.**
This cure focuses your mind on your objective: to attract love. The
red letters symbolize passion; the wooden box encourages growth.

Tie a red ribbon around your bedpost.
The lucky red ribbon used in this cure reminds you of
your intention to enhance your love life.
Each time you look at it, you put energy toward that objective.

**Tie two *I Ching* coins together with a red ribbon
and place them near your bed.**

Two is the number of partnership. *I Ching* coins, held
together by a lucky red ribbon, help strengthen a
bond between you and a romantic partner.

**Tie two rings together with a red ribbon
and put them on your nightstand.**

Like the above cure, this remedy combines circles (which represent
harmony) with red (luck, passion). Rings are powerful symbols of love
and commitment, so they strengthen the effectiveness of this cure.

Hang a picture of two swans in your bedroom.

Swans mate for life, so they are a good images to focus on if you want to strengthen the bond between you and a lover.

Place a pair of dove figurines in your bedroom.

Doves are symbols of peace and harmony. In China, birds are also seen as harbingers of good luck, so including a pair of ceramic, glass, or metal doves in your bedroom can enhance a relationship.

Display the number 2 in your bedroom.

Two is the number of partnership, so displaying the numeral in your bedroom reinforces your objective—to attract a partner or enhance an existing relationship—at a subconscious level.

Place a 2-foot-long piece of red ribbon under your mattress.
This cure combines two symbols—the number two and the color
red—to add passion to your love life.

Place a red or pink star in a spot where you'll see it often.
The star is a symbol of hope. Red and pink are colors we connect
with love, so this cure combines both symbols to help you keep a
positive attitude about love and relationships.

**Remove photos of friends, family members, and people
other than you or your romantic partner from your bedroom.**
Pictures of other people draw your attention to them and distract
your energy away from your romantic partner.

Remove broken jewelry from your jewelry box.
Broken objects suggest breaks or impediments, so fix or get rid
of broken jewelry to avoid breaks between you and a partner.

**In your bedroom, place an image of the animal that
corresponds to the Chinese year in which you were
born together with an image of your partner's animal.**
These two animal figures are powerful symbols of you and
your partner. Let them help to enhance your relationship.

Display the *I Ching* pattern "Tui" in your bedroom.
This symbol connotes joy and a harmonious exchange
between two people who nourish each other. Each time you
look at it, you are reminded of your intention to strengthen
the connection between you and a partner.

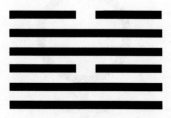

Display the astrological symbol for Venus in your bedroom.
Like the previous cures, viewing this planetary symbol of
love reinforces your intention to increase the amount
of love in your life.

Hang a circular wreath in your bedroom.

Circles represent unity, harmony, and infinity. This remedy combines the power of the geometric shape with a wood cure (plants) to enhance your love life. For best results, hang a wreath made of dried roses.

Hang a circular mirror in your bedroom.

The circle promotes harmony, and the mirror opens up new possibilities. For best results, position the mirror so it reflects your bed or an object that signifies love and partnership to you.

In your bedroom, place a small figurine of a deity or personage who represents love, such as Venus, Aphrodite, or Cupid. On a psychological level, this cure impresses a powerful image of love on your subconscious. In an esoteric sense, you are inviting a deity to help you improve your love life.

Hang a yin/yang symbol in your bedroom. This symbol, shown on page 150, depicts masculine (yang) and feminine (yin) energies united and balanced.

Put a dark blue object on your dresser or nightstand.

This is a good cure to use when you want to resolve an argument or reach an agreement because dark blue facilitates compromise and can improve communication between you and a partner. For best results, choose an item that is vase-shaped or round. A perfume bottle made of cobalt blue glass is ideal for this purpose.

Place a rose-quartz egg on your nightstand.

This cure is good for couples who want a child because it combines the loving vibrations contained in rose quartz with the ovoid shape that symbolizes fertility and new life.

Put a red or pink tablecloth on your dining table.
This cure encourages you to nurture yourself with love.
Red and pink are colors we connect with romance,
so use them as a visual trigger when you eat.

Place two pieces of rose quartz side by side on your dresser.
Rose quartz contains subtle vibrations that affect the emotions to
strengthen feelings of affection. This cure also uses the number
two to encourage affection between you and a partner.

Shine light into dark corners in your bedroom.

Dark corners sap positive energy and can have a depressing affect
on a romantic relationship. Light up your love life by positioning a
lamp so that it illuminates a dark corner of your bedroom.

Set a small piece of quartz crystal in your bedroom window.

Quartz crystals reflect light—and ch'i. They also hold and increase
the energy of your intention, so placing one in a bedroom window
can brighten your romantic prospects.

Move your bed out from under a slanted ceiling or eaves.

A slanted ceiling depresses ch'i and limits its positive influence. If your bed is positioned under eaves or a slanted ceiling, the amount of love you receive may be restricted. Move the bed to another location.

Hang a small mirror on a slanted ceiling or eaves.

If you can't move your bed to another spot in the room, hang a small mirror (preferably a round one) on the ceiling above your bed to symbolically open up the ceiling.

Leave the door to your bedroom open during the day.

This allows ch'i to circulate into your bedroom throughout the day, so your love life doesn't stagnate.

Keep the bathroom door closed.

If a bathroom is located across from or adjoining your bedroom, close the door to keep ch'i from flowing down the drains and dampening your love life.

Don't put a TV in your bedroom.

A TV brings influences from the outside world into your private space and distracts you from your intention

to create a romantic environment.

Cover your TV when it isn't in use.

If you can't put the TV elsewhere, cover it with an attractive piece of cloth when it isn't in use to minimize its influence on your love life.

Don't put your computer in your bedroom.

A computer focuses energy on work and distracts your attention from romance. Move it to another area in order to improve your love life.

Cover your computer at night.

If you must keep your computer in your bedroom, cover it with a cloth at night to separate your work from your personal life.

Fill a pottery jar with rice and place it in your bedroom.

This cure is for people who want to have children. Both rice and the earth element are associated with fertility; when combined, they increase your chances of conceiving.

**Fill a wooden bowl or box
with seashells and set it on your nightstand.**
This is a good cure for a man who wants to attract a woman or for
couples who want to have a child. Shells symbolize the water
element (which nurtures all living things) and feminine energy.
Wood encourages growth. For best results, use nine
shells because this is the number of fulfillment.

Use a wooden headboard to promote growth in a relationship.
The wood element encourages expansion and growth, so use this cure
to attract a partner or enliven an existing relationship.

Use a metal headboard to strengthen commitment.
The metal element increases concentration, focus,
and stability in a relationship.

Place a lamp with a metal base on your nightstand.
Like the above cure, this one uses the metal element
to strengthen the commitment in a relationship.

**Place a lamp with an earthenware or
porcelain base on your nightstand.**
This cure uses the earth element to increase your level
of trust, comfort, and security in a relationship.

Place a lamp with a glass base on your nightstand.
This cure encourages better communication
and cooperation between you and a partner.

Put a small stone in each of the four corners of your bedroom.
Stones are symbols of stability and permanence,
so this cure is a good one to use if you want to increase
the level of trust and security in a love relationship.

Good Luck and Happiness

Put a higher wattage light bulb in your home's entrance area.
Think of how uneasy you feel entering a dark foyer or hallway.
Adequate lighting in your entrance area will attract ch'i into your
home—and make visitors feel welcome, too.

Sweep your front steps, porch, or sidewalk.
Like clutter, accumulated dirt, dead leaves, and other natural
debris make the entrance to your home unsightly and
can interfere with the smooth flow of ch'i.

Attach shiny brass numerals to your front door.

Ch'i enters your home through the front door. But first you have to attract ch'i and get it to come to your home instead of passing right by. To do this, make your front door attractive and distinctive.

Polish the numbers on your front door.

If you already have numbers on your front door, polish them—and while you're at it, polish your door knob and door knocker, too. The more appealing your front door is, the more ch'i you are likely to attract. The physical act of improving your entryway's appearance also helps you to focus on your goal.

Hang a mirror between your home and oncoming cars.

This one is good for people who live near a street. Do the headlights of oncoming cars shine into your windows? This situation can produce feelings of uneasiness. Hang a small mirror outside your window so that it faces oncoming traffic and reflects the stressful energy back in the direction of the street, away from your home.

Position a mirror on your roof.

Use this cure if you live next to a tall building that dwarfs your home. Placing a mirror on your roof deflects the oppressive energy of the larger building away from your home.

Hang a wreath on your front door.
This cure makes your home's entrance more attractive.
A circle symbolizes harmony, so placing a wreath on
your door encourages congeniality and happiness.

Change the decoration on your front door each season.
This gesture not only keeps your entryway looking attractive, it
acknowledges the changes in nature and life to help align you with
the Tao and the earth's cycles.

**Tie nine small bells on a red cord and hang
them on the inside of your front door.**

Each time you enter your home, the pleasing sound of bells tinkling encourages you to think happy thoughts. The sound of the bells also gently stimulates positive ch'i and breaks up stagnant energy. Nine is the number of fulfillment and red is a lucky color, so this combination of symbols attracts happiness and luck to your home.

**Hang two bells on the doorknob of your front door,
one on the inside and one on the outside.**

Like the above cure, the pleasing sound of the bells prompts positive thoughts each time the door is opened. By hanging a bell on each side of the door, you encourage happiness and good fortune in both the personal and public sphere.

Hang a wind chime in your foyer.

Moving objects activate ch'i and circulate it throughout your home. This cure is good to use in a small, windowless, or self-contained entry (such as a mudroom) where ch'i can get stuck.

Place a vase of fresh flowers in your entryway.

Flowers are not only an attractive accent in your home, they symbolize growth and life. Place these in your entrance area to attract good luck and happiness.

Place a circular, glass bowl or jar near your front door.

This provides a place for you to put your keys, sunglasses, and other items that you take with you when you leave the home. Symbolically, circles represent harmony and glass improves communication between the inhabitants of the home.

Hang a circular mirror in your entrance area.

This cure is both practical and symbolic. The circle encourages harmony, the mirror reflects and increases light. A mirror in this spot also enables you to check your appearance before you go out.

Place an attractive area rug in your entry area.
This gives an instant impression of warmth, comfort,
and welcome. It also creates a focus for ch'i, drawing and
holding positive energy in your home. For best results,
choose a golden, brown, tan, or russet rug.

Illuminate a stairway clearly.
This cure is particularly beneficial if your home has a split-level
entryway. When ch'i encounters this situation, it becomes confused
and doesn't know which way to go. Direct ch'i by illuminating the
portion of the split stairway that you want it to follow.

**Hang pictures or decorative objects
on a hallway wall in a foyer with a staircase.**
If your foyer has a steep stairway, ch'i may enter and go
immediately up the stairs, instead of circulating through your
home. Hang pictures or decorative objects on the wall of the hall
to attract ch'i's attention and slow down its movement so that you
receive its benefits in all areas of your home and life.

Place a large plant under steps with open risers.
Ch'i can slip through steps with open risers instead of flowing
smoothly from one floor of your home to another.
To keep this from happening, place a large plant under
the stairs to catch and elevate the ch'i.

Hang a mobile under steps with open risers.

Like the above cure, this one keeps ch'i from slipping through steps with open risers. The mobile circulates positive energy from one floor of your home to another to enhance your happiness and good fortune.

Hang a wind chime at the end of a long hallway.

If your home has a long entrance hall with the front door at one end and the back door at the other, facing each other, hang a wind chime in front of the back door to circulate ch'i back into your home keep it from departing too quickly.

Place a large plant at the end of a long hallway.
This cure performs a similar function to the one above. The large
plant keeps ch'i from entering your home and rushing
right out the back door.

To the right of your front door, hang a map of a place you want to go.
In feng shui, the area to the right of your entryway is associated
with travel. Use this cure if you want to take a trip.

Enter each room of your home every day.
If a room is unused, the ch'i in it grows stale. To activate the
positive flow of ch'i and keep your life from stagnating, walk
through every room in your home at least once each day.

Hang a mobile in an unused room.

This stirs up "stuck" ch'i that can stagnate in a room that isn't used regularly. Touch the mobile whenever you enter the room to set it in motion and activate the cure.

Turn on a light in an unused room.

Illuminate an unused room for at least ten minutes each day to activate ch'i and keep it from stagnating.

Place a live plant in an unused room.

The living plant keeps ch'i activated an unused room. When you tend the plant, which symbolizes growth, you energize the room and stimulate the flow of positive ch'i.

Wash a window in your living room.

Light—and ch'i—stream into your home through the windows.
Clean windows allow more of both to enter your living space
and brighten your life.

Wash a mirror in your living room.

Make sure a mirror is clean and that the silver backing is in good
condition so that it reflects perfectly. A dirty or damaged mirror
suggests murkiness or lack of clarity in your social or family life.

Replace a burned-out light bulb in your living room.

A burned-out light bulb diminishes the amount of ch'i in your living room and can limit your happiness or good fortune, especially where friendships and family life are concerned. Something that doesn't function properly symbolizes damage and obstacles.

Vacuum or dust the lampshades in your living room.

Dirty shades dim the amount of light generated by your lamps. Keep them clean to allow ch'i to brighten your friendships and family life, and bring you good luck.

Place three throw pillows on your sofa.

Three is the number of activity and change, so this cure is a good one
to use if you want to stimulate your social life or meet new friends.

Keep closet doors closed.

Closets represent the private side of your life, because this is where you
store things out of sight when they are not in use. Keep closet doors
closed to prevent personal matters from becoming public knowledge.

Don't position a sofa under an exposed beam.

Overhead beams depress ch'i and produce a sense of heaviness. If your sofa is positioned beneath an exposed beam, you may experience pressures or burdens in your family or social life. Move the sofa to a more favorable location.

"Soften" an exposed beam.

If you can't move your sofa, "soften" the influence of the exposed beam by draping it with fabric or hanging plants on it.

**Hang a photo that signifies friendship
to the right of your front door.**
Feng shui connects this spot with friendship and congenial
associations with other people. If you want to expand your circle
of friends and acquaintances, hang a photo of a group of friends
or a happy social occasion to the right of your front door.

**Place an image of your Chinese zodiac animal
in a prominent place in your home.**
There are twelve animals in the Chinese zodiac. Your special animal
serves as a protector and guide, bringing you good luck and happiness.

Place a small figurine of a laughing Buddha in your living room.
The Buddha is the most revered deity in the East. Choose an
image of him laughing to attract happiness to your home.
Sometimes the Buddha is shown carrying a sack over his shoulder;
the sack contains all your troubles, which he has gathered up—a
very fortunate symbol to feature in your home.

Hang a yin/yang symbol in your living room.

This symbol depicts the harmonious blending of masculine (yang) and feminine (yin) energies, and represents balance.

Display the *I Ching* hexagram
"Feng" in a prominent place in your home.
This figure means abundance or fullness and invites the three
Chinese blessings—health, wealth, and happiness—
into your home, and your life.

Display the astrological glyph

for the Part of Fortune in a prominent place.

This symbol represents good fortune and success. Displaying it in
a place where you'll see it often reminds you of your goal to attract
good luck and happiness in all areas of your life.

Ring a bell in the corners of your living room.

This cure stirs up "stuck" ch'i that can collect in the corners of a room and chases away any "bad vibes" that may have accumulated.

Burn incense in your living room.

Incense combines the elements fire and air, and gently stimulates positive ch'i. Lighting incense is also an ancient method for conveying prayers to the heavens.

Burn nine candles in your living room.

This fire cure stimulates positive ch'i while also creating a pleasing ambiance. Nine is the number of fulfillment.

Place a live plant in your living room.

Plants provide a decorative touch, while
symbolizing growth, life, and well-being.

**Put a pebble, a seashell, an acorn (or pine cone),
and a key in a red container and set it in your living room.**

This cure combines all five elements to encourage balance and good luck.

Include all five elemental colors in your decorating scheme.

The five colors are red (fire), yellow (earth), black (water),
white (metal), and green (earth). Combine these colors
to create balance in your home.

**Hang a picture in your living room
that includes all five elements in it.**
This cure promotes balance and good luck.
(Refer to the Elemental Table on page 9 for specifics.)

**Hang a picture in your living room
that contains a mixture of yin and yang colors.**
This cure helps to balance your living area and encourages harmony in friendships. Blue, green, and black are yin colors; red, orange, yellow, and white are yang. Purple is already a blend of yin and yang (blue and red).

Don't let clutter accumulate on your dining room table.
Clutter corresponds to discord and obstacles. If it collects on
your dining room table, tension or problems may arise
between members of your household.

Place a bamboo flute or other bamboo item in your living room.
The Chinese consider bamboo to be a lucky plant because it can
grow up to 40 inches per day. Bamboo flutes, in particular, are
believed to have the ability to lift heavy or depressing energy.

Hang a wind chime between you and a noisy neighbor.
Wind chimes disperse unpleasant vibes and circulate them away
from your home. Hang one in a window facing your neighbor's
property to break up negativity so it doesn't disturb you.

Hang a faceted crystal ball in a window between you and a neighbor.
This cure is similar to the one above. The faceted
crystal ball catches and breaks up energy coming from
a neighbor, so it doesn't affect you so strongly.

Hang a wind chime between your home and the street.
Use this cure if you live on a busy street. The wind chime
disperses disruptive street noises before they get to your home.

Hang a mirror between you and a bad view.

If the view from one of your windows is less than ideal, hang a mirror in the window so that it faces the unpleasant view and symbolically reflects the unwanted energy from that vista away from your home.

Hang a mirror between your home and a nearby building.

If you live next to a building that's very close to your home, you may feel crowded by it. Hang a mirror outside a window facing the other building to deflect the oppressive energy of the tall building away from your home.

Place a piece of quartz crystal in your living room window.
Quartz crystal augments whatever it touches. Because ch'i enters
your home through the windows, you can increase its positive
effects by placing a chunk of crystal on the windowsill where it
will catch and amplify sunlight.

Smudge antiques and used objects to purify them.
Objects that have been previously owned by someone else can retain
the vibrations of other people and places. Therefore, it's a good idea to
cleanse antiques and other used items. Use the smoke from burning
incense or dried sage to "smudge" and purify pre-owned articles.

Smudge your living room.

Use the smoke from burning incense or a bundle of dried sage to cleanse your living room of unwanted energies. Do this once each season. You can also smudge your home after an argument or unpleasant incident to remove "bad vibes."

— Health / Well-Being —

Position your bed so that when you are in it
you can easily see the entrance to your bedroom.
When you can't see the entrance to your bedroom, you may
subconsciously feel anxious that someone could enter and startle
you. This uneasiness can interfere with restful sleep.

Hang a mirror so when you are in bed you can
see the entrance to your bedroom reflected in the mirror.
Use this cure if you cannot position your bed
so that you can easily see the door.

If your bed is positioned beneath an overhang or slanted ceiling, hang a small mirror on the ceiling over your bed.

A slanted ceiling or overhang depresses the ch'i above your bed and can lead to headaches or other physical ailments. A mirror symbolically "cuts a hole" in the ceiling to alleviate pressure.

Hang bamboo flutes on an exposed, overhead beam in your bedroom.

Bamboo is considered lucky in China and flutes are believed to have an uplifting effect. If you can't move your bed, hang two bamboo flutes on the beam so that the mouthpieces point down, to lift up the depressing ch'i.

Move your bed away from a window.

Drafts from a window may lead to a cold or flu. From the perspective of feng shui, ch'i enters your home through the windows and can overwhelm you if your bed is directly in front of a window.

Move your bed if it shares the same wall as a toilet.

If your bed is on the same wall as the toilet—even if they are on opposite sides of the wall—your vital energy may disappear down the drain while you sleep. Move the bed to another location.

Clean under your bed.

Dirt, clutter, and disarray interfere with the smooth flow of ch'i—
and healthful energy—through your home. Dust and clutter under
your bed can disrupt your sleep.

Put green or blue sheets on your bed.

These colors have a calming effect
and can help you relax so you sleep better.

Ring a dinner gong before eating.

In China, gongs are sometimes rung before meals to chase away
unwanted energies so you can eat in peace and harmony.

Ring a bell in the corners of your bedroom.

Pleasant sounds clear the air in your bedroom and chase stagnant ch'i away, so it doesn't interfere with your sleep or diminish your vitality.

Increase the amount of light in your bathroom.

The prevalence of water in bathrooms tends to create an abundance of yin energy, which can sap your vitality. To balance this situation, add more lights or use higher-wattage bulbs in your bathroom.

Place a live plant in a sick room.

Because plants signify health, life, and growth, they can attract positive energy to an ailing person and aid many health conditions.

Place white flowers in a sick room.

White is associated with purity and protection in many cultures, so white flowers can be beneficial for people with contagious diseases or those whose immune systems are fragile.

Place red flowers in a sick room.

Red adds a touch of the fire element and can help boost the vitality of someone whose natural energy has been weakened by illness. (Note: Red isn't a good choice for people with high blood pressure, because it can be too stimulating.)

Place purple flowers in a sick room.

Purple combines yin (blue) and yang (red) in equal parts, creating a balanced blend of these two energetic forces. Therefore, purple flowers can help restore balance to an ailing person's system.

Hang a mobile in the bedroom.

This cure is good for clearing congestion and respiratory problems because it keeps ch'i circulating through the room.

Display the *I Ching* symbol
"T'ai" in a prominent place in your home.
This hexagram represents peace. Hang it where you will see it
often and be subconsciously encouraged to achieve peace, balance,
and well-being in all areas of your life.

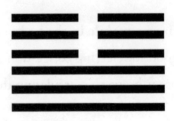

Display the astrological glyph for the Sun near your front door.
The Sun provides the vital energy necessary to support life on earth.
Therefore, its symbol can be a powerful, subconscious motivator,
encouraging you to lead a healthy lifestyle.

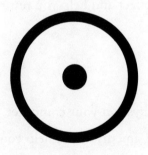

Display a green star in a place where you'll see it often.
The star is a symbol of hope. Green represents new growth and healing.
This cure combines both symbols to promote health and well-being.

Place a piece of amethyst on your nightstand.
The soothing vibrations in amethysts can have a
calming effect and help you rest peacefully.

Place a piece of amethyst on your computer, desk, or workstation.
The calming energy of amethysts can help you handle stress at work.
Pick up the stone and hold it whenever you feel tense.

Place a piece of tourmaline on your computer.

Tourmaline absorbs electrical emissions from your computer that
might cause stress or otherwise damage your health.

Burn incense in the center of your home.

Feng shui associates the center of your home with health.
In many spiritual traditions, incense is used to send prayers to deities.
Burn it in the center portion of your home and let its smoke
carry requests for good health up to the heavens.

Place a light in the center of your home.

Ch'i is attracted to light, so this cure helps to increase vitality.

CHAPTER 5

CURES YOU CAN DO IN A DAY OR LESS

THE CURES IN THIS CHAPTER will take a

bit longer to implement than those in the previous chapter, but you can complete most of them in less than a day. Some require a bit of technical skill or a few familiar tools. Among these cures I include decorating advice, home repair suggestions, and gardening options.

As in chapter 4, the cures are grouped into four categories: Prosperity, Love, Good Luck and Happiness, and Health/Well-Being. Many of the cures work best if they are implemented in the room(s) that relate to the area of life you wish to influence, as discussed in chapter 2. I briefly explain the feng shui philosophy and symbolism behind each cure to help you understand how and why these techniques work. Because some cures are more applicable to some situations than others, I also describe which conditions the cures are designed to correct.

Like the cures in chapter 4, these remedies should start to work quickly, however, it may take a while before you see the results—especially you are trying to rectify a situation that has existed for a long time. I suggest that you choose a few cures and put them in place, then wait a couple of weeks before doing anything else. During that time, pay attention to the changes that are taking place in your life and your responses to these changes. You may want to keep a journal of the process.

If the cures you've enacted don't work as quickly or as effectively as you'd hoped, try a few more. Feng shui offers so many solutions that you usually have several options that will serve your purposes and be suitable for your particular situation.

Prosperity

Clean your stove.

Your stove generates wealth and money-making opportunities. A dirty stove puts obstacles in your way and limits your earning capabilities.

Clean out your refrigerator.

Clutter causes obstructions and confusion. When you remove stale or spoiled food from your refrigerator, you symbolically open up space for prosperity to enter and fresh opportunities to fill the gap.

Clean out under your kitchen sink.

Like the above cures, this one removes confusion and obstacles associated with clutter, leaving space for new opportunities and prosperity to come your way.

Clean your office of all clutter.

Clutter that accumulates on your desk and in other parts of your office creates obstacles to your prosperity. Clearing away clutter also improves your comfort level and your efficiency, so you are more productive at work.

Organize floppy disks, CDs, and other disks, et cetera.

Like the previous cures, this one improves your efficiency and removes obstacles that can delay or interfere with your financial success.

Take care of "Post-it" notes.

These constant reminders of things you haven't done yet can distract you from the task at hand. They also make you feel inefficient or overwhelmed by unfinished business. Tend to them quickly so they don't interfere with your productivity and sense of accomplishment.

Clear your in-box.

Like the previous cure, this one clears up matters that can cause distraction and diminish your productivity. Completing this task enables you to be more efficient and stay on top of work-related issues.

**Get rid of outdated magazines,
trade journals, manuals, and other materials you aren't using.**

Old magazines and journals are associated with outmoded thinking. To encourage new ideas that can generate wealth, remove outdated materials from your office.

Install an aquarium and put nine goldfish in it.

Nine is the number of fulfillment. Water, which nourishes all life, is associated with prosperity. And the goldfish connection is obvious.

Decorate your office or work space with
upholstery fabric, drapes, wallcovering, or carpeting
that combines eight colors or patterns in the design.

Eight is the number of business and finance, so this symbolic cure reminds your subconscious that your goal is to make money.

Take clothes that no longer fit to a consignment shop.

This cure brings you money when you sell what you no longer
need. It also eliminates old things that can keep you stuck
in the past and opens up space in your life for new money-making
possibilities to come your way.

Paint your office door red or purple.

These colors are considered lucky in China. Painting the door to
your work area red or purple attracts fortunate people, rewards and
recognition, and opportunities that can advance your career.

Paint your office door green or black.

Black is the color of money in China. Green is associated with
growth and in some countries it is the color of paper money.
Therefore, these colors can help you increase your income.

Use fire colors—red, orange, gold—
in your office to spark enthusiasm and creativity.

Fire cures help to stimulate and inspire you. Best used as accents or
in small amounts, these colors can get you out of a rut, increase
your vitality, and jump-start your income.

Paint your office green to encourage financial growth.

Green, the color of healthy plants, is associated with growth. In some countries, it's also the color of paper money. Use this color cure to boost your income. A calming color, green also reduces stress.

Paint your office blue to reduce stress.

This cool, calming color can help you keep your cool under pressure. As a result, you become more efficient and focused, which can increase your earning potential.

**Paint your office gray to strengthen
your clarity and sense of purpose.**
Gray helps you focus on your goals and strengthens
your resolve to accomplish what you set out to do.

Paint your kitchen white to save money.
Because this color is connected with the metal element, it increases
your determination and tenacity. Wealth is generated in the kitchen,
so this is a good cure to use if you have trouble holding on to money.

Use accents of red or orange in your kitchen.
Fiery colors increase the amount of ch'i in your kitchen and can
augment your finances. Psychologically, these colors stimulate
appetite. Too much fire, however, can cause stress, so it's best to
use these bright hues in small doses.

Place a wooden table and chairs in your kitchen.
Wood, because it comes from living trees, is connected with
growth. Wooden furniture in your kitchen can help you increase
your income. For best results, use a rectangular table.

Adjust doors in your kitchen and office so they open and close easily.
Anything that doesn't work properly impedes the smooth
flow of ch'i, creating an annoyance for you and compromising
money-making opportunities. Plane the edges of doors
that stick, oil hinges, fasten wobbly knobs, et cetera.

Cook meals at home regularly.
The stove generates wealth, but only if you use it. You can increase
your prosperity by preparing home-cooked meals often.

Repair nonfunctioning burners on your stove.
The stove is a source of wealth, but if its burners
don't work properly your ability to make money will be limited.

Repair a broken or damaged piece of furniture in your office.

Broken objects relate to broken deals, contacts, promises, or dreams. To prevent financial losses, repair or replace broken or worn furnishings in your work area.

Create a "money tree."

This creative project helps you focus on your money-making objectives. Draw a tree—a feng shui symbol of growth—and place pictures of items you want to acquire on its branches. Display your money tree prominently.

Set up a prosperity altar in your home.

Collect an assortment of objects that symbolize wealth to you and arrange them on a table, shelf, or other prominent place. This prosperity altar focuses your intention and draws money into your home. For best results, hang a mirror behind your altar so that it reflects the items you've selected and "doubles" their power.

Wear red to attract fame and career success.

This dynamic fire color increases your chances of being noticed. Wearing it also strengthens your self-confidence and can help you push forward with your career goals.

Wear dark blue or black to inspire confidence.

These colors give the impression of seriousness and dignity. Therefore, they cause other people to see you as someone they can trust and rely on. Dark blue and black also facilitate communication, so these are good colors to wear if you must speak publicly, conduct a meeting, or work in a communications field. Combine dark blue or black with white for best results.

Wear light blue to help you stay cool under pressure.

Light blue enhances serenity and helps
you handle stress, so you can work more effectively.

Wear green to attract money and encourage hope.

Green is the color of springtime and new growth.
In some countries it is the color of paper money, so wearing it
can help you to improve your financial situation. Green also
encourages feelings of hope in you, so this is a good color to
wear when you are dubious about your chances of success.

Wear brown to stay grounded.

The color of the earth, brown helps you keep your
feet on the ground and improves your ability to handle
financial matters in a practical manner.

Wear white to improve concentration.

White enables you to focus clearly on the task at hand
and improves mental clarity. Wear white to take tests or tackle
difficult mental tasks successfully.

**Make the area to the right of your
office's entrance as visually appealing as possible.**

Feng shui connects this area with people who can help you in your
career or money-making efforts. Use attractive furnishings, artwork,
or plants to enhance this spot and attract helpful people.

Repair a leaky or malfunctioning toilet.

This cure keeps money from leaking away.

Install attractive faucets on your bathroom sink.

This cure helps keep ch'i (and money) from flowing
away too quickly. Ch'i, attracted to the handsome faucets,
will pause momentarily before going down the drain.

Plant evergreen shrubs at the entrance to your home.

Because they keep their greenery all year, evergreens are a powerful
symbol of lasting wealth. Plant one or more near your
front door to enhance your finances.

Set a pair of stone lions near your front door.

The lion is the king of beasts and a symbol of royalty.

Set a pair of lion figurines near the entrance to your home,

to provide a positive image and help you attract wealth and power.

Install a birdbath in your yard.

Feng shui connects water, which nurtures all life, with

money. Birds are also considered lucky, so this cure combines

both symbols to increase prosperity.

Install various types of lighting in your office or work space.

A combination of task and ambient lighting allows

you to direct light—and ch'i—on your objectives.

Install track lighting on an exposed beam in your office.
Heavy beams compress ch'i and hold down its
beneficial properties. This cure uses the fiery energy of
electric lighting to diminish the depressing influence of a heavy
beam so it doesn't limit your earning ability.

Put a wooden desk in your office or work area.
Wood, because it comes from living trees, is connected
with growth. Using a wooden desk in your office or work
area can help you increase your income.

**Position a bookcase to the left of your
office door and fill it with books.**
In feng shui, this spot is associated with wisdom and learning.
Put your books here to increase your knowledge or help
you improve your skills so you can earn more.

Decorate your office with fabrics that have triangles in them.
Triangles stimulate activity. Choose fabrics for
upholstery, drapes, or carpeting that feature this
shape to spark new money-making opportunities.

Place a rectangular area rug in your office.
Rectangles symbolize growth because they are longer
than they are wide. A rectangular area rug in your
office encourages financial growth.

Place a thick, plush rug in your office.
Plush, richly textured carpets—particularly ones made of wool—
symbolize prosperity. As part of the earth element, a
thick rug can help you hold onto money, so this cure is
good for people who have trouble saving.

— LOVE —

**Install a dimmer switch on your bedroom lamps
so you can adjust light levels to suit your mood.**
Soft lighting is romantic and restful. Light also influences
the intensity and movement of ch'i, so adjusting the amount
of light in your bedroom enables you to increase or
decrease the amount of energy in the room.

Paint the door to your bedroom pink or red.
This cure, which uses the colors associated with affection
and passion, invites love to enter your life.

Use accents of red or pink in your bedroom.

If red or pink walls in your bedroom would seem
overwhelming, use accents of these colors to attract new love
or enhance romantic feelings in an existing relationship.

Paint your bedroom a dark color.

Dark colors create a sense of intimacy, so they are good choices for a
bedroom if you want to deepen your connection with a partner.

Paint your bedroom green.

This cure is good for nurturing loving feelings in a new
relationship because green is the color of growth. It can
also encourage harmony in an existing partnership.

Decorate your bedroom with a combination of yin and yang colors.
This color scheme establishes balance in your love life because it blends yin (feminine) and yang (masculine) energies. Combine blue, green, or black (yin) with red, orange, yellow, or white (yang). Purple is already a blend of yin and yang (blue and red).

**Clean out your jewelry box and remove
any jewelry that has associations with a past partner.**
Gemstones and metals hold on to the vibrations of people who have handled them. Additionally, anything that reminds you of a past relationship can interfere with your receptivity to a new partner.

Place jewelry that you connect with past relationships in a box and tie it with a red ribbon.
If you can't bring yourself to sell or give away jewelry that reminds you of a previous partner, use this cure to symbolically make peace with that person from your past and let it go so you can move on to another relationship.

Organize shoes neatly in your closet.
Shoes are symbols of support as well as our connection with the ground. To attract a supportive and well-grounded relationship, organize your shoes neatly. Get rid of those that don't fit or that are worn, outdated, or unappealing.

**Place old love letters, photos, or mementos
of past relationships in a box and tie them with a red ribbon.**
If you can't bring yourself to let go of old mementos, use this cure
to symbolically put them behind you and let go so they don't block
new love from coming to you.

**Remove from your bedroom all books, equipment,
projects, and materials that relate to other areas of your life.**
If you keep objects and equipment that remind you of work or
other areas of your life in your bedroom, they can distract you
from your intention to enjoy a fulfilling love relationship. Move
them to another, more appropriate part of your home.

Repair a damaged or worn piece of furniture in your bedroom.

Broken objects can symbolize broken dreams or promises;

worn items suggest boredom or diminished enthusiasm.

Fix damage so it doesn't damage your love life.

Adjust the door into your bedroom so that it opens and closes easily.

A door that doesn't open properly makes it harder for ch'i to enter

your bedroom and activate your love life. Adjust the door so it opens

smoothly, to smooth out the sticky areas in your relationship.

Adjust a window in your bedroom so that it opens and closes easily.
Anything that doesn't function properly in your bedroom indicates an area that isn't operating smoothly in your love life. This cure helps to remove sticky situations and frustrations in a relationship.

Plant a rose bush in your yard.
Roses are symbols of love. By planting one, you are symbolically planting your intention to attract a new relationship or nurture an existing one. Each time you look at or tend the rose bush, you'll be reminded of your objective.

**Plant flowers in a window box and
install it at your bedroom window.**
This cure is similar to the previous one. Choose flowers
that remind you of love—red or pink ones are best.

**Include in your bedroom at least
one piece of furniture that has curved lines in its design.**
Curved lines and rounded shapes symbolize promote harmony
and cooperation, so they are good to use in a bedroom. S curves,
such as those found on Queen Anne and Victorian furniture,
can help improve communication with a partner.

Place a round area rug in your bedroom.

Circles symbolize harmony, so this cure

encourages congenial feelings between you and a partner.

Place a rectangular area rug in your bedroom.

Because rectangles encourage growth, this cure is best for people

who are seeking a new partner or who want to increase affection in

an existing relationship. Couples who want to have a child could

also use this cure to increase fertility.

Position furniture in your bedroom so that each piece rests on the rug.
In this arrangement, the rug brings all the room's furnishings
together, symbolizing connection and harmony between the
various aspects of a love relationship and the people involved.

Eat with wooden chopsticks.
This cure combines the number two with the wood element to
encourage love to grow between you and a partner. It also enhances
your ability to nurture each other.

Include fabrics with circular patterns in your bedroom.
This cure uses the symbolism of a circle
to promote unity and wholeness in a relationship.

Decorate your bedroom with fabrics that have two colors in the design.
In this cure, the number two, which symbolizes a union of complementary energies, helps to promote harmony in a love relationship.

Decorate your bedroom with fabric that features a flame-shaped pattern.
Flame-shaped designs, like triangles, encourage action
and excitement in your love life. Choose fabric with this
shape for curtains, bedspread, upholstery, or accent pieces.

Decorate your bedroom with soft, luxurious fabrics.
Materials with pleasing textures—such as silk,
cashmere, or Egyptian cotton—appeal to your sense of touch.
This cure works by stimulating your senses.

Decorate your bedroom with a balance of coarse and smooth textures.
This cure blends yin (smooth) and yang (coarse) materials to create
balance and happiness in your love life.

Tie a broken blue heart with a red ribbon.
This cure helps to heal a broken heart. Fashion a blue heart out of
clay, paper mâché, wax, or another material, then break it into two
pieces. Tie the pieces together again with a red ribbon. Put the
heart in a drawer in your bedroom.

Frame pictures in metal frames.

Use this cure to strengthen the commitment between you and a partner. The metal element is associated with permanence and stability. For best results, frame two pictures in matching frames.

Frame pictures in wooden frames.

The wood element promotes growth, so use this cure to increase loving feelings in an existing relationship or to attract a new partner. For best results, frame two pictures in matching frames.

Put a few drops of rose, jasmine, ylang-ylang, or musk
essential oil in the tub and take a long, hot, luxurious bath.
These scents are associated with love and passion,
so inhaling them while you bathe stimulates feelings of affection.

Rearrange your bedroom furniture annually.
To keep your love life from getting stale, move the furniture in your
bedroom each year to stir up ch'i and excitement.

Good Luck and
— Happiness —

Install a light fixture near your front door.

Helpful ch'i must be able to find your home before it can enter and energize it. If no light exists near your front door, install one. This also provides safety and welcomes you and visitors to your home.

Repair a broken light fixture.

If the light near your front door is broken or burned out, it's worse than not having one there at all. Broken or nonfunctioning objects represent obstacles, limitations, and disruptions in your life, so fix damage to avoid hindering your good fortune.

Trim shrubs near your home's entrance.

This enables ch'i to reach your home easily, without encountering obstructions that could limit its beneficial energy.

Plant flowers, shrubs, or other plants near your home's entrance.

If you don't already have plants near your entrance, this cure can help attract ch'i to your home and encourage growth and good fortune in all areas of your life. Window boxes or ceramic planters are good choices for apartment dwellers.

Plant white flowers in front of your home for security.

White is the color of protection, so this cure is an attractive way to provide security for your home and family.

**Plant golden-yellow flowers to encourage
optimism and attract friends.**

Yellow, the color of the sun, sends out positive signals and encourages feelings of optimism. Therefore, golden-yellow flowers in front of your home give the impression that you are a cheerful person. In China, this color is associated with spirituality and intelligence, so you could attract people who embody these qualities.

Install an attractive mailbox near the entrance to your home.

This cure makes a positive statement about you as the
occupant of the home. It also attracts the attention of
ch'i and keeps it from passing by your home.

Hang a prayer flag in your home.

In Buddhism, prayer flags are hung to attract blessings. These flags are usually printed with written prayers and images of benevolent deities. Sometimes they incorporate the five colors associated with the five Chinese elements, to promote balance and harmony. You can purchase ready-made prayer flags or make them yourself. Hang your flag inside or outside your home. When the wind catches it, your prayers are carried on the breeze to a favorite deity while also sending blessings to everyone the wind touches.

Install a light to complete a "missing corner."

Use this cure if your home is L shaped. In feng shui terms, an L shaped home is "missing" a section and this can cause bad luck. To visually extend the corners of your home to "fill in" the missing section, install a light where the imaginary corner would be.

Use a shrub or potted plants to complete a "missing corner."
This cure functions like the previous one. A shrub or
large potted plant can be used to fill in a missing corner.

Install a birdbath or shrub between your home and oncoming traffic.
If your home is located at the end of a dead-end street or a
T-shaped intersection, you may subconsciously feel threatened
by the strong energy of oncoming cars. To neutralize this, place
a birdbath or shrub between your home and the street,
creating a psychological barrier to protect you and
deflect the energy of approaching traffic.

**Put up a metal or white fence between
your home and oncoming traffic.**

White is connected with the metal element, and metal is known
for its strength, so this cure gives you protection from traffic, both
physically and psychologically. It's especially useful for people who
live at the end of a T-shaped intersection or a curve that puts them
directly in the line of approaching cars.

Paint your entrance area golden yellow.

Yellow is the color of the sun, so it represents the sun's life-giving
energy and warmth. Associated with the earth element, golden yellow
promotes comfort and stability. This cheerful color is also welcoming
to guests and makes a good first impression.

Place eye-catching objects at intervals throughout your home.
This encourages ch'i to slow down as it moves through your home,
focusing first on one thing, then another, so that positive energy flows
smoothly throughout the entire area.

**Replace a broken pane of glass in a
living room or dining room window.**
Broken, worn, or damaged objects represent areas of your life
where problems exist. A broken windowpane fragments ch'i as it
enters your home and reduces its positive impact.

By replacing a broken pane of glass, you psychologically
demonstrate your willingness to correct problems and symbolically
allow positive ch'i to enter your home undamaged.

Wash all the windows in your home.

Because ch'i enters your home through the windows, this cure allows more positive energy to stream into your home and bring you good luck.

Wash all the mirrors in your home.

The reflecting power of a mirror is diminished and distorted by dirt. Clean all your mirrors so they function optimally and generate good fortune.

Fix a door in your living room that doesn't open or close properly.

Doors that stick, creak, don't stay shut, or have loose doorknobs can interfere with the smooth flow of ch'i in your home. Damaged or malfunctioning items also represent areas of your life that aren't operating properly. Oil hinges, plane edges, and fasten doorknobs securely.

Install, replace, or fix door locks.

Nonexistent, flimsy, or improperly functioning locks produce feelings of insecurity. Install new locks or repair existing ones so they work properly.

Repair a crack in your living room ceiling or wall.

Cracks in the structural features of your home can undermine areas of your life. In your living room, they can cause splits between friends, colleagues, and people with whom you socialize or interact regularly.

Repair a worn or broken piece of furniture in your living room.

Worn or damaged furniture in your living room can have an adverse effect on your social life and cause discord among the people who live in your home. Repair or replace broken items to restore happiness.

Clean out and organize a closet in your living room.
This cure makes room in your life for more congenial
relations between members of your household, with friends,
and with other people in general.

Clean your fireplace or wood stove.
A dirty fireplace or wood stove is both inefficient and unsafe.
On a symbolic level, this condition can limit your vitality,
enthusiasm, and good luck.

Clean out your attic.

Like other organizing cures, this one reduces blockages and confusion that clutter produces while also opening up room for good luck and opportunities to come into your life. The attic of your home symbolizes your mind and spiritual life, so clearing the attic helps clarify your thinking and beliefs.

Clean out your basement.

This cure is similar to the one above. The basement represents your subconscious, so this cure can help you deal with repressed issues or past conditions that haven't been resolved yet.

Clean out your garage.
Like the above cures, this one helps you eliminate confusion, obstacles, and old behavior patterns and habits. It also clears the way for new opportunities and good luck to enter your life.

Sweep cobwebs from the corners of your home.
Cobwebs and dust are symbols of the past. Clear away "stuck" energy by sweeping your corners clean.

Weed your garden.
Weeds suggest that problems are choking your growth and limiting good fortune. Pull them out to remove impediments to your happiness.

Trim house plants.

This general maintenance task encourages plants
to grow healthy and bring you good luck.

**Clear all the halls, stairs, and walkways
through your home of clutter.**

Obstacles in the passageways through your home
block the smooth flow of ch'i and the many benefits it brings.

Organize CDs, tapes, and records.

This cure reduces confusion, clutter, and discord in your life.

Put loose photos in an album.

Like other organizing cures, this one helps clean up
confusion and clutter in your life. Looking at photos can
also prompt happy thoughts and memories.

Organize magazines, books, and newspapers.

Get rid of any reading materials that are out-of-date or no longer
useful to you. Old books and magazines clutter up your space, keep
you stuck in the past, and prevent new ideas from emerging.

Return borrowed items.

Objects that belong to other people hold the energetic vibrations of their owners. This decluttering cure enables you to clear their energy (and any distraction it could cause) from your home. It also lets you check off something on your "to do" list and remove any lingering guilt or annoyance you might feel if you've kept these items too long.

Hang crystals in all the dark corners of your home.

This cure brightens your life by shining light into shadowy, "gray" areas and removing darkness that can dim your spirits.

Ring a bell in the corners of each room of your home.

This cure stirs up "stuck" ch'i that can collect in the corners
of your home and chases away any "bad vibes" that have accumulated.
Do this ritual once each month.

Put two or three small area rugs in a long hallway.

If your entrance hall is long and narrow, use two or three small rugs
instead of a runner to create distinct areas. This will slow down ch'i
and keep if from rushing too quickly down your hallway.

Install a ceiling fan in your entrance hall or living room.

Fans stir up "stuck" ch'i and circulate it into
other parts of your home, so it nurtures every facet of your life and
encourages activity in your social life.

**Arrange the furniture in your living room so that,
when seated, no one's back is to the room's entrance.**

A person seated with his or her back to the entrance
can't see when someone enters the room and, consequently,
may feel anxious or vulnerable. You create a more comfortable,
secure environment by positioning seating so everyone
can easily see the entrance to your living room.

Reposition furniture that obstructs easy access to a room.
A piece of furniture that blocks traffic into or through the
room is an inconvenience to you and obstructs the smooth
flow of ch'i. Move any pieces that jut into walkways,
interfere with opening doors, et cetera.

Arrange living room furniture in a triangular pattern.
Triangles are stimulating shapes, so you can increase the amount of
activity in your social life by positioning furniture, such as a sofa and
two chairs, in a triangular configuration.

Arrange living room furniture in a rectangular configuration.

Rectangles encourage growth and expansion, so use this furniture arrangement to attract new friends and rewarding social experiences.

Position living room furniture in a square arrangement.

Squares represent stability and permanence.

Arrange furniture in a square configuration to encourage security and grounding in the social or domestic sphere.

**Use a large area rug in your living room
to bring family members together.**

Use this cure if your home's occupants don't interact as much as
you'd like them to or if discord exists between family members.
Place a large area rug so that all pieces of furniture in your living
room sit on it. The rug "connects" the separate items to symbolically encourage family togetherness.

Rearrange the furniture in your living room annually.

This cure keeps your social life from growing stale and encourages
new relationships, experiences, and ideas.

**Decorate your dining area or living room with a
combination of yin and yang colors.**
This color scheme establishes balance in your living area and bodes
well for harmonious friendships with people of both sexes. Combine
blue, green, or black (yin) with red, orange, yellow, or white (yang).
Purple is already a blend of yin and yang (blue and red).

**Decorate your living room with a
balance of coarse and smooth textures.**
This cure blends yin (smooth) and yang (coarse)
materials to encourage balance and happiness.

Install an aquarium in your living room.

Aquariums grace many Chinese restaurants and are considered good luck. Because fish are living creatures, they are apt symbols of life, health, and growth, and water nourishes all living things. An aquarium also makes a colorful, calming addition to your interior environment.

Paint your living room yellow, peach, or pink.

These colors enhance sociability and optimism.
Use them in your living room to animate your social life.

Paint your living room green or blue.

Use these colors if you want a calmer, more peaceful existence.

Set up an altar to attract happiness and good fortune.

Position your altar in a place of honor and set items on it that suggest happiness to you. Be sure to include representations of all five Chinese elements on it. You might also choose to feature a figure of the Buddha, Kwan Yin, or another deity whose blessings you wish to attract.

Place representations of the five elements in your yard or garden.

Include objects that bring together the five elements to create balance and harmony. Some possibilities are a distinctive stone or clay flowerpots (earth), a bowl of water or a birdbath (water), a crystal or lantern (fire), a piece of metal outdoor furniture or metal wind chime (metal), and of course plants (wood).

Hang nine pictures in your living room.

Nine is the number of fulfillment, the most auspicious number.

Display pictures that convey happy images.

**Include nine pieces of furniture (or a combination of furniture
and accessories such as lamps) in your living room.**

This cure taps the lucky energy in the number nine.

Ideally, you'll want to include a variety of shapes, materials,
and textures to feature all the elements.

Smudge your home.

Use the smoke from burning incense or a bundle of dried sage to cleanse your home of unwanted energies. Do this once each season. You can also smudge your home after an argument or unpleasant incident to remove "bad vibes."

Eat at a kitchen or dining table with a glass top.

In feng shui, glass is linked with communication and flexibility. Eating meals on a glass-topped table can help improve communication and cooperation among members of your household.

Decorate your living room with glass-topped occasional tables.
Like the above cure, this one promotes good communication. When tables with glass tops are placed in the social areas of your home, they encourage lively rapport among family members and guests.

Decorate your living room with marble-topped occasional tables.
This cure uses marble, which represents the earth element, to encourage comfort, security, and stability in your home.

Eat meals at a round dining or kitchen table.
Because circles are symbols of harmony and unity, this cure enhances congenial feelings between family members.

**Position a round rug in your dining room
so that the table and all chairs are on the rug.**
This cure uses the symbolism of a circle to promote cooperation
and unity among household members. A rug that connects all
pieces of furniture also brings people together.

Place a round or oval area rug in your living room.
Circles symbolize harmony, so this cure encourages
congenial feelings among household members and guests.

Place a rectangular area rug in your living room.
This cure is good for people who want to expand their circle
of friends and acquaintances, because rectangles promote growth.

In your living room, include one or more pieces of furniture with curved shapes.
Curved shapes—and particularly S curves such as those found on Victorian and Queen Anne furniture—encourage communication, give-and-take, and adaptability. When positioned in your living room, they promote positive interactions between household members and guests.

Use fabrics with nap or nubby textures in your living room.
Velvet, wool, suede, and other richly textured fabrics suggest comfort and warmth. Decorate your living room with these materials to promote grounding and security.

Put last season's clothes away
as soon as they are no longer appropriate.
Don't allow clothing from the previous season to occupy a prominent
place in your closet—store it away or move it to the back of your
closet instead. This cure keeps you from getting stuck in the past.

Wear purple to enhance spiritual pursuits.
This color is linked with spirituality in the West
and with good fortune in China. Wearing it can help you
in your search for truth, wisdom, and meaning in life.

Hang a red cord so that it stretches from ceiling to floor.
The cord in this cure symbolically channels blessings from heaven
(ceiling) to earth (floor). Red is considered a lucky color, so position
this cure in the area of your home that corresponds to the part of your
life in which you want good luck and blessings.

Hang wind chimes on all four corners of your home.
This cure dispels harmful or disruptive energy
and guards your home at every direction.

— Health / Well-Being —

Replace a broken pane of glass in a window.

The windows of your home are like your eyes—
you see the outside world through them. Cracked or broken
panes of glass can lead to eye problems.

Install adequate lighting at your front door.

This enables you and visitors to see clearly when they enter
your home. Light also directs ch'i into your home.

Repair broken steps or loose railings at your home's entrance.
Damaged steps, porch railings, et cetera pose safety hazards. They
also damage the quality of the ch'i that enters your home.

Fix cracked or broken pavement in a driveway or sidewalk.
Like the above cure, this one has both a practical safety component
and a symbolic one. Repair a damaged sidewalk or driveway to
attract ch'i and prevent accidents.

Clean under your bed and store items elsewhere.

Articles stored under your bed can interfere with restful sleep because they remind you, subconsciously, of whatever they symbolize. Check to see what's under your bed and what symbolism is attached to these items. Get rid of anything you don't need and store the rest neatly in another place.

Clean out a closet in the center of your home.

The center of your home corresponds to health. If your home has a closet in this spot, keep it neat and organized to avoid confusion, blockages, and other problems with your health.

Balance the five elements in the center of your home.

Create a harmonious combination of fabrics, shapes, colors, and other features in the center of your home to encourage good health. (Refer to the Elemental Table on page 9 for more information.)

Repair a dripping faucet or toilet that runs or leaks.

A leaky faucet or toilet drains off positive ch'i and depletes your energy.

Decorate your bathroom with fiery colors.

The presence of so much water in the bathroom causes an abundance of yin energy. Balance this condition by decorating your bathroom with warm red, orange, or golden yellow.

Use straight lines your bathroom.

This cure also balances the abundance of yin energy in your bathroom. Choose fixtures, furniture, and accessories with straight lines and angles instead of curving shapes.

Paint your bedroom white.

White is associated with purity and protection, so this is a good color to use in the bedroom of a person who has delicate health.

Paint your bedroom blue.

Blue is a calming, soothing color. Use it in your bedroom to promote feelings of serenity and encourage restful sleep.

Decorate your bedroom with complementary colors.

Use complementary colors to create a balanced and harmonious environment, to encourage proper rest and rejuvenation. Balance red or pink with green, blue with orange, purple with yellow.

Rearrange furniture in your bedroom annually.

This cure keeps ch'i from getting stuck, where it can cause sluggishness, congestion, or other health problems. If someone is suffering from an illness, rearranging the furniture in that person's bedroom can stir up ch'i and help promote a change in his or her condition.

"Soften" an exposed beam above your bed.

Exposed beams compress ch'i and can cause health problems.
If a heavy beam is above your bed and you can't move your
bed to another location, reduce the depressing influence
of the beam by draping it with fabric or red ribbon,
or affixing dried or silk flowers to it.

Build a rock garden outside your home.

A rock garden promotes stability and security. Building it provides
good exercise and helps to focus the mind. A rock garden is also an
ideal place to sit and relax or meditate.

**Perform a "blessing" ritual before having a
tree in your yard cut down.**

Changes in your yard, as well as inside your home, affect the
movement of ch'i and can have an impact on your health. If you
must have a tree trimmed or cut down, feng shui recommends
doing a blessing ritual beforehand to avoid health problems. The
tree's trunk and limbs are symbolic of your own and it isn't
uncommon for people to suffer ailments related to the part of the
tree that has been cut. Fill a glass with red wine (or water dyed
with red food coloring). Beginning at the east, walk clockwise
around the tree while sprinkling wine around its base until you
have completely traced a circle. After the tree has been trimmed or
taken down, cover the exposed cut. A good permanent solution is
to plant ivy so it will grow over the stump.

ABOUT THE AUTHOR

Skye Alexander is also the author of two astrology books, *Magickal Astrology* and *Planets in Signs*, and the mystery novel *Hidden Agenda*. She has also written for radio, television, magazines, newspapers, and anthologies. For more than a dozen years, she worked as an interior designer and has been using feng shui since 1987. She lives in Gloucester, Massachusetts, with her cats.